Celtic Mythology

DON NARDO

LUCENT BOOKS

A part of Gale, Cengage Learning

GALE
CENGAGE Learning·

Farmington Hills, Mich • San Francisco • New York • Waterville, Maine
Meriden, Conn • Mason, Ohio • Chicago

LIBRARY OF CONGRESS CATALOGING-IN-PUBLICATION DATA

Nardo, Don, 1947-
Celtic mythology / by Don Nardo.
     pages cm. -- (Mythology and culture worldwide)
Includes bibliographical references and index.
ISBN 978-1-4205-0923-6 (hardback)
1. Mythology, Celtic--Juvenile literature.
BL900.N37 2014
398.2089'916--dc23

2014014954

Lucent Books
27500 Drake Rd.
Farmington Hills, MI 48331

ISBN-13: 978-1-4205-0923-6
ISBN-10: 1-4205-0923-3

TABLE OF CONTENTS

Map of the Celtic World

Legend:
- Celts Today
- Celts in History
- Influence

ISLE OF MAN
PICTS
SCOTS
IRISH
North Sea
Baltic Sea
WELSH
CORNISH
BRITTANY
Rhine R.
Loire R.
Danube R.
Alesia
(SYTHIA)
Atlantic Ocean
GAULS
KELTOI
La Tene
Hallstatt
KELTOI
Lyon
Po R.
Danube R.
Marseilles
Black Sea
CELTIBERIANS
Telamon
BALKANS
Rome
Pergamon
ITALY
GREECE
GALATIANS
Delphi
ASIA MINOR
Athens
Carthage
NORTH AFRICA
Mediterranean Sea

Family Tree of the Primary Tuatha De Danann (the leading race of Irish Celtic gods)

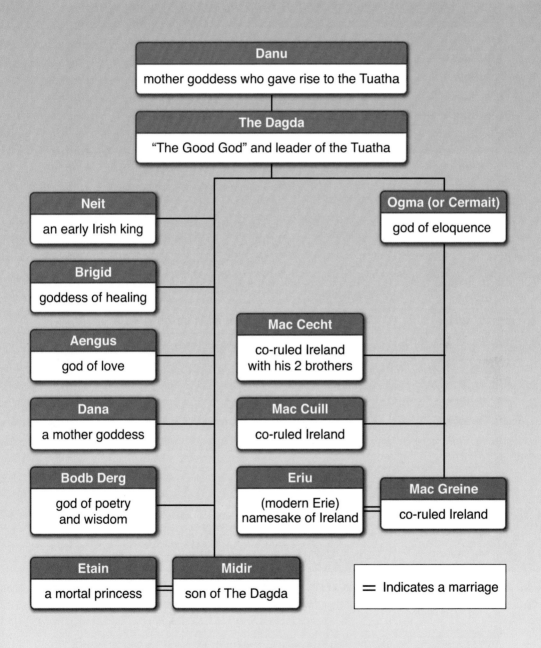

Danu
mother goddess who gave rise to the Tuatha

The Dagda
"The Good God" and leader of the Tuatha

Neit
an early Irish king

Ogma (or Cermait)
god of eloquence

Brigid
goddess of healing

Aengus
god of love

Mac Cecht
co-ruled Ireland with his 2 brothers

Dana
a mother goddess

Mac Cuill
co-ruled Ireland

Bodb Derg
god of poetry and wisdom

Eriu
(modern Erie) namesake of Ireland

Mac Greine
co-ruled Ireland

Etain
a mortal princess

Midir
son of The Dagda

= Indicates a marriage

Major Entities in Celtic Mythology

Character Name	Pronunciation	Description
Andraste	an-DRAH-stee	A Romano-Celtic war goddess favored by the first-century A.D. British warrior queen Boudicca.
Arthur	AR-ther	The famous mythical Welsh or English king who, with his chivalrous knights, held court in the fabulous castle of Camelot.
Bran	BRAWN	A Welsh god who saved his sister Branwen from the clutches of an evil Irish king.
Branwen	BRAWN-wen or BRAN-oo-wen	A Welsh goddess who married an Irish king who ended up abusing her.
Brigid	bri-GEED	An Irish goddess of healing who allowed a wild boar to live within her sacred compound.
Cuchulain	koo-HOO-lin	An ancient Irish warrior-hero who transformed himself into a frightening super-soldier just prior to battle.
Culhwch	kil-HOOKH	An ancient Welsh hero who had to perform a series of difficult tasks in order to win the hand of the woman he loved.
Étaín	ay-DEEN	An Irish princess who was changed into a tiny fly by a witch but was later reborn in human form.
Finn McCool	fin-m'KOOL	A great ancient Irish hero known for leading a band of hunters known as the *fiana*.
Guenivere	GWEN-uh-veer	The wife of King Arthur and queen of Camelot.
Lancelot	LAN-si-lot	The French knight who became one of King Arthur's greatest knights but betrayed Arthur by having an affair with the queen.
Lugh	LOO	An ancient Irish god thought to be an inventor or master of various arts and crafts.
Matholwch	math-OH-lookh	The wicked Irish king who mistreated his new bride Branwen, thereby incurring the wrath of her brother Bran.
Merlin	MER-lin	The mysterious magician who tutored the young King Arthur.
Midir	MID-ear	An Irish deity who searched high and low for the woman he loved, Étaín, and eventually found her.
Olwen	AHL-wen	The woman whose father forced the hero Culhwch to perform various tasks in order to be worthy of marrying her.
Peredur	peer-ah-DEAR	An old Welsh Celtic spelling of King Arthur's knight Percival, known for searching for the sacred Grail.
Rhonabwy	row-ON-a-bwy	A medieval knight who had a dream about King Arthur in an old Welsh myth.
Tuatha De Danann	TOO-ah d'DAH-nan	The main family of ancient Irish gods.

Three Basic Celtic Questions

O f the world's many and diverse collections of surviving ancient myths, that of the Celts is among the most colorful, appealing, and universally beloved. Celtic mythology almost literally overflows with entertaining characters and situations. In the memorable words of noted scholars Kathryn Hinds and Francine Nicholson, "With exciting plots, strong characters, and an aura of magic and mystery, the mythological tales of the Celts make for terrific storytelling." In these stories, "warriors careen in chariots across the landscape and leap out to engage in single combat" and "heroes travel through fog and mysterious caves." Meanwhile, "masters of magic, women and men alike, weave enchantments around people, animals, objects, and landscapes."[1]

Celtic mythology is also extremely accessible, more so than many other world mythologies. Those seeking to enjoy more than a passing glance at its vivid, lively legends require relatively little basic background information. Indeed, practically everything needed to get started with the Celtic myths can easily fit into a nutshell containing the answers to three fundamental questions.

Separated Yet Similar

First, who exactly were the people who created these myths? That is, were the Celts all members of one homogeneous national group or culture, like the modern Japanese? Or were they members of separate cultures tied together by a number of shared beliefs and customs?

Evidence unearthed by archaeologists and historians strongly suggests that the Celts did not spring from a single biological stock. In other words, they did not hail from and revere a specific ancient founding ancestor or family. Instead, they belonged to an assortment of tribal units that had in common a number of beliefs, values, and other cultural elements.

Up until the middle of the twentieth century, relatively little was known about that culture and the everyday lives of the ancient Celts. But recent advances in technology have improved excavation methods. That has allowed archaeologists and historians not only to uncover more new data about the Celts, but also to reinterpret older finds, thereby revealing them in a fascinating new light.

For a long time, for instance, the assumption was that the Celts were a fairly primitive people. Or at least they were primitive compared to their famous and highly cultured neighbors—the ancient Greeks and Romans. Today, however, experts think Celtic society was quite complex and admirable in its own right. The Celts' values, beliefs, and means of expression were simply different from, rather than inferior to, those of the Greeks and Romans.

Connections Among the Celts

It is now known that the Celts developed out of what archaeologists call the Hallstatt culture, named for a lake of that name in northern Austria. Thriving from about 850 to 450 B.C., its members were illiterate but successful farmers and traders. They operated on the fringes of the more southerly Greco-Roman world that ringed the shores of the Mediterranean Sea.

Over time the Celts spread outward from their initial homeland, settling in regions as distant as Ireland in the west and what is now Turkey in the east. On the surface, these far-flung Celtic groups were often very different, culturally speaking. University of Wales professor Juliette Wood points out:

> No single set of cultural characteristics can adequately sum up what is meant by "Celtic" civilization. Celtic societies developed in response to a wide range of historical and geographical circumstances. In some areas, the Celts depended primarily on trade, but in others, the main activity was farming or stock breeding. Likewise, some groups were dominated by warrior elites or princely aristocracies, while others formed hybrid cultures with local ethnic groups.[2]

Despite such differences, certain ideas and customs were the same or almost so in all of the Celtic regional enclaves. These similar cultural niches included building techniques, religious concepts, tools, weapons, and fighting methods. Still another connection among the various Celtic groups was that they all spoke dialects of a shared ancient language. As late as A.D. 500—about the time of Rome's fall and the start of Europe's medieval period—a Celtic tribe in eastern Europe spoke a tongue that on the surface sounded very different from that of a tribe in faraway Britain. Yet both languages were derived from and exhibited numerous basic features of the one spoken by the residents of the original Hallstatt homeland.

Were Celtic Myths Universal?

Having determined that the Celts were separated into regional groups that shared certain cultural traits, one confronts the second basic question about Celtic mythology. Namely, where did its most popular tales—the ones that survived and continue to entertain people today—come from? Did they derive from just one local Celtic group—for instance, the Irish one? Or were these myths recognized and perpetuated by Celts everywhere?

It turns out that convincing evidence points toward universal recognition of the major Celtic myths throughout the ancient Celtic world. As in the case of the Celtic languages, on the surface each separate regional group seemed to have its own gods. Also, as was true in all ancient societies, the attributes and exploits of these gods were the primary basis for a society's sacred stories, or myths.

Yet although each Celtic group had some local deities unique to it, certain gods were worshipped throughout the Celtic world and in almost identical ways. Among these divine beings so widely held in common were sky gods, mother goddesses, and deities connected to various arts and crafts. Some valuable information about one of them was recorded by the renowned Roman military general Julius Caesar. In the 50s B.C. he invaded Gaul, what is now France, then a major Celtic region. During the conflict, Caesar dutifully observed his enemies' culture, including their gods and religious beliefs. "The god most worshiped by them is Mercury," he wrote. "And very many images of him are to be seen. They regard him as the inventor of all the arts, the guide on every road and on every journey, and the god who has most power in connection with money-making and commercial undertakings."[3]

Caesar called the god in question Mercury because it had numerous features like those of the Roman deity of that name, a patron of craftspeople, traders, and travelers. In the Celtic lands the god was called Lugh, Lugus Lleu, Visucius, and many other names, depending on the particular region or tribal group. Celts everywhere viewed him as the inventor or master of arts and crafts, as well as the god of knowledge and prophecy. Moreover, all Celtic groups had myths relating to that deity, as well as to other widely worshipped gods and human heroes.

Beliefs and Customs in Story Form

The fact that all Celts held some key legendary figures and tales in common begs the third major question about Celtic mythology. It asks whether the Celtic myths either reflected or influenced the beliefs, values, and customs of everyday life in Celtic society. Based on abundant literary and archaeological evidence, the answer to that question is a resounding yes.

Among the more colorful examples of the connection between Celtic myths and Celtic life is one that involves

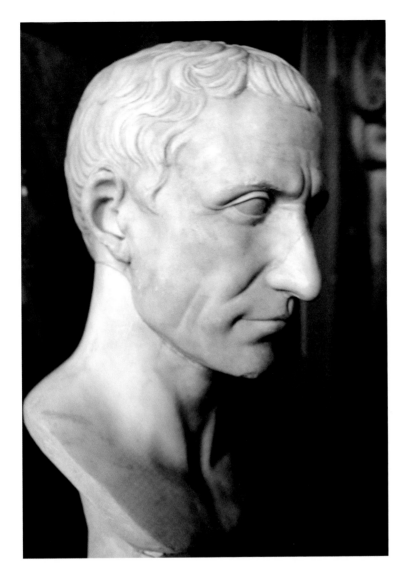

Roman general Julius Caesar wrote about the customs and religions of the Gauls after he invaded their lands in the 50s B.C.

a legendary character popular throughout the modern world—King Arthur. He is best known as a medieval English king who ruled a fabled land where heroic knights performed righteous deeds. However the earliest stories about Arthur emerged from an ancient Celtic society, specifically the one that long thrived in Wales, in southwestern Britain. Thus, at first he was a Celtic rather than an English character. As a result, many of the cultural aspects of his legendary world were based on ancient Celtic traditions and customs, not medieval English ones.

A clear example is the way a central facet of the charming story of Arthur's famous mythical sword, Excalibur, echoes a real ritual practiced by ancient Celtic warriors in the British Isles. In the traditional myth Arthur obtained the enchanted sword from a mysterious sorceress who dwelled beneath the surface of a lake. Years later, when he was mortally wounded in battle, he ordered one of his knights to hurl the weapon back into the lake. "This stirring tale contains a grain of truth," says researcher Laura Foreman. "Hundreds of Celtic swords have been recovered from pools, lakes, and bogs." Moreover, she writes, "Most of the blades were notched, broken, or [bent]. Scholars believe this may have been done deliberately, as a kind of ritual killing of the swords upon the deaths of their warrior owners. The now useless blades were then sacrificed to the waters, where they lay undisturbed until modern times."[4]

Was this quaint practice based on some very old mythical tales? Or perhaps it was the reverse—that the ritual came first and inspired the legend. The problem is that the myth emerged so long ago that there is no longer any way to tell which was older, it or the custom. What is more certain is that Celtic mythology contains a number of ideas and practices that correspond to or reflect actual aspects of Celtic culture. "Those who carefully examine all the evidence," Hinds and Nicholson point out, "find that the myths sometimes contain information that accurately depicts social conditions and behavior."[5]

Experts caution that one must be careful not to read *too* much into these ancient tales, since not everything in them reflects real life. Some aspects are clearly fanciful or meant to teach a moral lesson. But one of the chief purposes of all myths is "to express and pass on the values and beliefs of the people in story form,"[6] say Hinds and Nicholson. To that end, at the least, the surviving Celtic myths have succeeded in spectacular fashion.

CHAPTER 1

Customs and Lives of the Ancient Celts

N o one knows for sure exactly where the ancestors of the Celts came from. But the general consensus of modern archaeologists and historians is that they were part of a larger group of culturally similar peoples who many thousands of years ago occupied the vast steppes centered in what is now Ukraine, north of the Black Sea. They are generally referred to as the Indo-Europeans. This may be in part because their languages can all be traced back in time to a single tongue now called Proto-Indo-European.

Roughly five thousand to six thousand years ago (circa 4000 to 3000 B.C.), waves of these Indo-European peoples entered Europe. Some migrated southward and settled in Greece, where they imposed their language and culture on the more primitive folk who then lived there. Others moved farther westward into Italy, where various Latin-speaking tribes, including the early Romans, later arose. Still others spread into northern Europe, settling in what are now Germany and Austria.

Among these early northern European groups was one that settled near Lake Hallstatt, in the heart of the Salzburg Mountains (part of the larger Alps mountain chain), in Austria. The inhabitants of the region mined salt, which they called *hall*, a very valuable commodity they traded with

Distantly Related

While migrating across Europe and beyond in the 400s, 300s, and 200s B.C., the Celts did not realize that they were distantly related to the Greeks and Romans they encountered. All of these peoples were Indo-Europeans who had entered Europe in separate waves.

surrounding peoples. The salt was used not only to flavor food but also to preserve meat and as a base for a number of medicines.

Over time the community's leaders became wealthy, and the culture reached its zenith between about 800 and 450 B.C. Evidence for these facts comes from some two thousand tombs that archaeologists excavated in the vicinity of the lake in the twentieth century. Surrounding the skeletons in the grave sites were loads of finely made weapons, tools, pottery vessels, gold jewelry items, and other impressive artifacts. Experts came to call this society the Hallstatt culture and the roughly 350 years it thrived the Hallstatt period. They also came to view it as the first Celtic homeland. (In recent years a small minority of scholars has proposed an alternate theory. Based on genetic studies and other factors, they suggest that the Celts originated in northern Spain.)

From Traders to Settlers

Salt was not the only product that made the Hallstatt upper classes rich. Another was iron. In the early years of the Hallstatt period, these first Celts learned to extract iron from iron ore. Smiths beat the iron into a wide variety of shapes and items, among them swords, spear tips, cauldrons, axes, and farm implements. Use of such objects was a major innovation. "Iron-working transformed the Celtic world," scholar Jen Green points out.

> Iron tools worked better than ones made of bronze. Iron sickles and hoes—and later plows—made farming more efficient. Using iron axes, the Celts felled forests to bring more land under cultivation and to use the wood as building material and as fuel. . . . Iron also enabled the Celts to prosper as traders. By the seventh century B.C.E., they traded iron goods, along with minerals such as salt, copper, and tin.[7]

This ongoing, and at times long-distance, trade gave the Hallstatt Celts a growing awareness of the fertile and resource-rich European lands that existed beyond their own. As time went on they became increasingly less content to limit their contact with these areas to trade alone. Beginning in the 400s B.C., waves of Celtic warriors and settlers spread outward. Some moved along the Danube River into Hungary and surrounding areas. Others entered France, Spain, and Italy, while still others crossed the English Channel into the British Isles and occupied England, Wales, and Ireland. (It is important to realize that these migrants did not move into unpopulated areas, nor did they kill or displace the natives. As earlier Indo-European speakers had when seeking new homes, they became culturally dominant, imposing their

This ironwork was done by Hallstatt Celts. The Hallstatt culture was the first Celtic culture to smelt iron and make from it a wide variety of weapons and farm implements.

language and customs on weaker peoples who greatly out-numbered them.)

Rather than forming one big Celtic country or empire, how-ever, these new Celtic-ruled lands developed as separate societies with their own local leaders, customs, and goals. The main factors that tied them together were their similar language and culture and continued long-distance trade. In Laura Foreman's words, "As a loose collection of warlords and raiders, the Celts lacked a common goal, and would never display enough political unity to form an empire, or even a nation, preferring instead to render their allegiance to individual tribes."[8]

Many of these movements through central and north-ern Europe, especially those into Britain, were more or less invisible to the Greeks and Romans who lived farther south. Those Mediterranean peoples were well aware of the Celts' existence, however. The Greeks called them Keltoi (KEL-tee), and the Romans used both Celtae (KEL-tie) and Gauls to describe them. (The term *Gauls* came from *Gallia*, the Roman name for what is now France, where large numbers of Celts dwelled before the first century B.C.)

But it was not until groups of migrating Celts crossed the Alps into northern Italy in the late 400s and early 300s B.C. that Greco-Roman observers began to see them up close. As Oxford University historian Barry Cunliffe puts it, this was "the moment when Celtic peoples moved out of the obscurity of barbarian Europe into the brightly lit world of the Mediter-ranean, passing from prehistory to history."[9]

Reasons for Expansion

It remains uncertain exactly why the Celts migrated in enor-mous waves across Europe, changing the continent's history in numerous and major ways. Some ancient historians thought it happened at least partly because the Celts were attracted by the material riches of the Greco-Roman world, especially cer-tain luxury goods common to the Mediterranean lands. The first-century-A.D. Roman scholar Pliny the Elder, for example, stated that the Celts, whom he called Gauls,

> had as their chief motive for invading Italy, its dried figs, its grapes, its oil, and its wine, samples of which

had been brought back to them by Helico, a citizen of the Helvetii [tribe of Gauls], who had been staying at Rome, to practice there as an artisan. We may offer some excuse, then, for them, when we know that they came in quest of these various productions, though at the price even of war.[10]

Another theory suggested by ancient writers, including the first-century-B.C. Roman historian Livy, was that the Celts' expansion was due to a rapidly growing population in the Celtic homeland. According to this view, large groups of them started migrating in several directions, including into northern Italy, in the hope of reducing the numbers of tribesmen in central Europe. Although there may have been multiple reasons for the Celtic migrations, most modern experts suspect that population pressure was indeed the biggest contributing factor. Cunliffe writes that growing

Dealing with Surplus Population

One leading theory suggested by ancient writers to explain the Celts' expansion across Europe was that it was the result of growing population pressure in the Celtic homeland. One such writer was the first-century-B.C. Roman historian Livy. In describing how large groups of Gauls moved southward toward the Alps (which they later crossed on their way into northern Italy), he singled out a Gallic leader named Ambitgatus. Under his rule, Livy said,

Gaul became so rich and populous that the effective control of such large numbers was a matter of serious difficulty. The king, therefore, [sent] his two nephews, Bellovesus and Segovesus, both of them adventurous young men, out into the world to find such new homes as the gods, by signs from heaven, might point the way to. He was willing to give them as many followers as they thought would ensure their ability to overcome any opposition they might encounter. [Bellovesus collected] the surplus population [from the tribes] and set out with a vast host, some mounted, some on foot, and reached the territory of the Tricastini at the foot of the Alps.

Livy. *The History of Rome from Its Foundation.* Books 1–5 published as *Livy: The Early History of Rome,* trans. Aubrey de Sélincourt. New York: Penguin, 2002, pp. 379–380.

population, along with social demands for Celtic families to produce many children,

> could well have swelled their numbers. In such a turbulent and unstable situation, it would need only the decision on the part of one leader to take his [group] to the rich pickings of the south, for the news to spread, and others to follow, swelling the numbers to a migration and creating a momentum which drew in [even more people, causing] a rapidly escalating social upheaval.[11]

What Did the Celts Look Like?

Whatever the motives for their expansion, the migrating Celts intruded into numerous regions, always making a marked impression on the natives. Among those who put their observations of the newcomers in writing were several

The ancient Romans and Greeks depicted the Celts as being of large stature with white skin and blonde, reddish, or brown hair and having a warlike attitude.

Greek and Roman authors. Their accounts usually contained physical descriptions of Celts, which most often depicted them as white skinned with blond, reddish, or brown hair and having a large stature or fierce attitude—or both.

A classic example was the account of the fourth-century-A.D. Roman historian Ammianus Marcellinus. "Almost all Gauls are tall and fair-skinned, with reddish hair," he stated. "Their savage eyes make them fearful objects. They are eager to quarrel and excessively hostile." As for their voices, "most sound alarming and menacing, whether they are angry or the reverse. But all alike are clean and neat, and throughout the whole region [of Gaul], you will hardly find a man or woman, however poor, who is dirty or in rags."[12] Although Ammianus's description did fit many Celts, it certainly did not fit all. It is important to keep in mind that he and other Greco-Roman observers frequently presented caricatures (rough sketches or cartoon versions) of Celtic people and culture.

Meanwhile, despite how foreigners saw the Celts, they viewed themselves as reflections of the highly revered gods and heroes who inhabited their myths. It appears that the earliest Celtic storytellers assumed that those legendary characters were physically similar to themselves. The main difference was that the ancient gods and heroes were greater in stature and/or wore more magnificent clothes and armor than ordinary people.

Typical was a description of the mythical Irish hero Conall Cermach on his way to a contest of strength and bravery. It portrayed him as "a fair man with long wavy hair, a man of clear red and white complexion, wearing a white vest and a cloak of blue and crimson. His shield is brown, with yellow bosses and a bronze edge." Another legendary hero was depicted as "a big stout man, with reddish gold hair and long forked beard, dressed in purple with gold adornments; and his shield is bronze edged with gold."[13]

Different Rather than Inferior

Greco-Roman authors also devoted a fair amount of space to discussing Celtic society and customs, pointing out that the Celts were in large part culturally distinct from their Mediterranean neighbors. The Gauls and other Celts had no major permanent cities, for instance, as the Greek and Romans possessed in plenty. Instead, most Celts were primarily rural farmers and animal herders who dwelled in small villages and lived primarily off the land. Particularly damning in Greco-Roman eyes was the fact that the early Celts had no writing system to record their myths, religious beliefs, and political and social ideas.

The Greeks and Romans saw these cultural traits as extremely backward, which explains why they viewed the Celts they encountered as barbarians. Yet in truth, the Celts were far from uncivilized. They were no less experienced than the Greeks and Romans in the uses of iron, for instance. Also, Celtic societies had complex social organization and laws and well-developed religious beliefs and myths not unlike those in the Greco-Roman world.

Indeed, even in areas in which the Celts were supposedly culturally backward, their methods or approaches are better described as *different* rather than *inferior*. Their lack of literacy is a case in point. They amply made up for having no written documents by placing a greater-than-average emphasis on using memory to retain large quantities of information. In addition, they developed certain customs that made acquiring that information a way of strengthening family and community ties. Religious beliefs, memories of past events, and myths all passed from generation to generation orally through the art of local storytellers. As one noted scholar explains, this custom strengthened rather than weakened society:

> Listening to the tales of storytellers played a crucial part in everyday life. The stories provided a sense of the inherited past, they informed about the danger and temptations of life, and they provided a set of moral standards that the listener was invited to accept. No less important was the occasion itself—the coming together of family and friends sitting around the hearth engaged in the common pursuit of reflecting on their shared heritage.[14]

The faith that generated these orally preserved myths and religious beliefs recognized a great many gods. To interpret the wishes of those deities, as well as to maintain the mental storehouse of myths the storytellers drew from, Celtic

Written Caricatures of Celts

Experts point out that the numerous descriptions of the Celts and their culture by the ancient Greek and Roman, or classical, authors need to be taken with the proverbial grain of salt. Only some of these writers actually met any Celts in person, so their information was often secondhand. Moreover, even those writers who did observe individual Celts up close tended to use them as models for all Celts, as well as to accept rumors and stereotypes about them that to at least some degree distorted the truth. One of the leading experts on the Celts, Barry Cunliffe, sums up the problem:

To a Greek or Roman, the Celts were war-mad, quick-tempered, and unreliable. They were large, fair, mustached, tattooed, and they rubbed lime in their hair to make it stand up. Their curious barbarian habits included drunkenness, intense superstition, and the desire to fight naked wearing only a gold torque [metal necklace] around their necks. As in all caricatures, there must have been some truth lying behind these generalizations, but it is important to remember that the classical view is biased and distorted. It comes down to us through a series of interpretive filters. The ancient Celts seen through Greek and Roman eyes are essentially a metaphor, a vision manipulated to reinforce a range of ideals and preconceptions, rather than to offer an impartial, scientifically factual description of a people.

Barry Cunliffe. "In Search of the Celts." In *The Celts*, by Nora Chadwick. London: Penguin, 1971, pp. 18–19.

society had a small but special class of priest-like characters called the Druids. They also acted as teachers and judges in legal disputes and were composed of both genders, although some evidence suggests their ranks contained fewer women than men. Julius Caesar mentioned them in his writings about the Celtic tribes he fought in Gaul, saying in part:

The Druids are in charge of religion. They are responsible for all sacrifices [to the gods], public and private, and they decide all questions of ritual. Great numbers of young men come to them for instruction, and the Druids are very greatly honored by their pupils. It is the Druids, in fact, who are the judges in nearly all disputes, whether between tribes or between individuals. In every case of crime or murder, or question of

Druids like this one served the Celtic peoples as teachers and judges, as well as leaders of religious services.

a disputed legacy or boundary, they are the people who give the verdict and assess the damages to be paid or received. Any individual or community failing to abide by their verdict is banned from the sacrifices—and this is regarded as the worst punishment that one can have. Those who are excommunicated in this way are counted as criminals and evildoers.[15]

The Celtic Social Ladder

The extraordinary amount of authority and influence wielded by the Druids explains why they occupied a very high rung on the social ladder. In fact, the Druidic class held almost equal sway with Celtic society's highest-ranking class. The latter was composed of the king and his handful of socially prominent, wealthy, and influential warriors, who formed the Celtic version of nobility. The ruler's authority was based partly on how many of these retainers, or key fighters personally loyal to him alone, he commanded. (Another word for retainer is *vassal*, which derives from the Celtic word *gwas*.)

A major way such retainers could be bound to the king was by owing him a debt for services rendered. He often provided them with protection from enemies or rivals, for example, and he gave them plots of land, often along with cattle to graze on it. Clearly, only an extremely wealthy individual could provide such services to already well-to-do individuals; therefore, wealth was another major basis for a Celtic ruler's authority.

The king and his retainers appear to have dwelled mainly in large hill forts, which the Romans called *oppida*. The remains of thousands of them have been found across northern Europe; some of the best preserved of these are in the British Isles. Most of these hill forts were erected using large stones and masses of packed earth, reinforced by long, thick lengths of timber. One of the more spectacular examples is Dun Aengus. It was built on the edge of a sheer cliff overlooking the Atlantic Ocean on the island of Inishmore, off Ireland's western coast. According to Juliette Wood, the fort

The hill fort of Dun Aengus (shown) was built on a cliff on an island off Ireland's west coast. It is an excellent example of the Celtic oppidum, *the Latin word for a fortified settlement.*

was "defended by a zone up to around 70 feet (23m) wide of densely packed limestone pillars." She continues:

> We might assume that their function was to slow down the approaching enemy, whether on foot or on horseback, by making access through the main fortress walls painful and slow. A single, narrow passage leads through this defensive stone forest to the outer and inner walls, each of which today stands to a height of 12 feet (4m)—we can only guess at their height when they were first completed. The innermost of these walls seems impenetrable.[16]

These kinds of seemingly impregnable forts were frequently depicted in Celtic myths. Often the stone-lined enclosures provided a hero and his companions refuge from hideous monsters that wanted to eat them. Conversely, according to some myths, in very early times powerful gods ruled the surrounding countryside from such hilltop structures. Both the fortresses and countryside were seen as parts of an Otherworld, a legendary realm that was invisible to the human senses. Celtic mythology is replete with tales of such peculiar places. Variously picturesque, strange, or frightening, they were thought to be inhabited by fairies, gods, ogres, and other nonhuman beings.

In the real world, meanwhile, ordinary Celts—farmers, fishers, weavers, laborers, and the like—usually lived outside the hill forts. They made up the largest social class, ranked on the social ladder well below those of the king, his retainers, and the Druids. Men and women were more or less equal in status and rights and often even fought in battle together. One important difference was that, with some notable exceptions—including several queens—men held society's top leadership positions.

The dwellings of these common folk were made from perishable materials, mainly wood, thatch (straw), and wattle and daub (a mesh of wooden strips held together by a glue-like mixture of clay, straw, and/or animal dung). Typically, a central upright post was connected to a ring of surrounding posts by long lengths of timber. Builders covered the dwelling's ribs with thatch and/or wattle and daub. A central stone

A typical Celtic Iron Age dwelling.

or brick hearth provided heat and a cooking surface, and the smoke escaped from a small hole cut in the ceiling.

The Celtic Cattle Raiders

Most people in Celtic society remained in whatever social class they were born into. However, men and women alike could enhance their personal status within their own class by performing various acts of prowess. These might include leading a military raid or collecting loot from an enemy during a raid

Celtic Women

Women in most ancient societies, including those of Greece and Rome, had fewer rights than men and were treated as second-class citizens. In contrast, Celtic women were nearly equal in status and rights to their fathers and husbands. Celtic society was essentially patriarchal, or male dominated, and most leaders were men. Yet the path to high authority was not completely blocked to women, who sometimes rose to positions of political power, including the roles of foreign diplomat and queen. (The most famous Celtic queen was Boudicca, of the British Iceni tribe, who led a large-scale rebellion against Rome in the first century A.D.) Also, some of the Druids, Celtic society's hugely respected high priests and judges, were women. In addition, women regularly fought in battle beside their husbands and served as mediators in tribal political disputes.

Meanwhile, women in all social classes enjoyed economic and legal rights and clout almost unprecedented for females in the ancient world. In an undetermined number of tribes, they were free to choose their own husbands during the Celts' pagan (non-Christian) centuries. (That right eroded quickly after the Celts converted to Christianity.) Women could also divorce their husbands at will and had various property rights equal to men's. "A woman was responsible for her own debts and not those of her husband," noted scholar Peter B. Ellis writes. "A woman could inherit property and remained the owner of any property she brought into marriage. If the marriage broke up, then she not only took out of it her own property, but any property her husband had given her during the marriage." Only after Celtic society had been long exposed to Roman culture and later to Christianity, both of which were very patriarchal, did female Celts begin to lose their near equality with men.

Peter B. Ellis. *Celtic Women: Women in Celtic Society and Literature.* London: Constable, 1995, pp. 94–95.

Celtic queen Boudicca led a rebellion against the Romans.

and distributing it to friends and associates. In fact, Cunliffe points out, evidence clearly shows that the custom of raiding and obtaining victory and booty was a "central focus of Celtic society," which was very war oriented. It was a system that was in a way self-perpetuating. Cunliffe adds:

> It is easy to see how the limited raid on neighbors would need to give way to more adventurous expeditions, and how, for some sectors of the community, raiding could have become a full-time occupation. In this context, the long-distance raid, requiring the absence from home for many months, becomes readily understandable.[17]

The manner in which military raiding became such an important social custom among the Celts is not completely clear. However, some scholars believe that myths played a vital role. Many of the raids in question were centered on a specific kind of loot or booty—cattle. As noted modern mythologist Bruce Lincoln concluded in a 1980 landmark study, cattle raiding was a common event depicted in Celtic myths. The most famous version comes from the Irish Celtic legend of the superhero Cuchulain, who was said to have conducted a classic heroic cattle raid.

The central role of cattle and cattle raiding in myths may have contributed to the similar role they played in Celtic society. Indeed, these animals were central to the Celts, as well as to many other Indo-European peoples. Celtic society viewed cattle as having great value and sometimes used cows as a form of currency with which to measure wealth, buy things, and pay debts. Therefore, cows were highly coveted items, and cattle raiding was common in all of Europe's Celtic regions.

The Celts viewed their own cattle raids as righteous and heroic because some of their gods and heroes had conducted such raids. In contrast, the thinking went, foreign peoples who stole from Celts were dishonorable, even immoral. "The point of the myths," scholar David Leeming writes, "seems to be that foreigners steal, while Indo-Europeans raid. The former activity is demeaning, [but] the latter is noble." In more contemporary terms, "bad raiders are terrorists, while good raiders are freedom fighters."[18]

The Prominence of Fighting

Conducting successful raids was not the only way the Celts improved or showed off their social status. Taking part in a pivotal, sometimes dangerous activity known as "the feast" was another. Such a gathering, which drew many of the warriors in a community or region, was not just a lavish meal. It was also a contest to identify the area's leading fighter. (The custom appears to have been limited to male warriors, but no firm evidence has yet been found indicating that women were excluded.) When the cow or other animal constituting the main course was served, one man stepped forward to claim the "hero's portion," usually consisting of the thighs. If no one challenged him, he was acknowledged to be that society's bravest warrior. However, if another man did dispute his claim, the two fought, sometimes to the death, to establish who was superior.

This custom is described in considerable detail in several Celtic myths, including an ancient Irish one titled Bricriu's Feast. In it Bricriu is a noted innkeeper in the region of Ulster (in northeastern Ireland). He holds a huge feast to which he invites all of Ulster's best warriors and then offers the hero's portion to three of them at once, knowing full well they will fight for the honor. The three heroes are the formidable Cuchulain; Conall Cermach, known for carrying the severed head of an enemy behind one of his knees; and the funny but deadly Loegaire Buadach. The three warriors fiercely attack one another until finally Cuchulain emerges the winner and claims the hero's portion.

The prominence of warriors and fighting in numerous Celtic myths was reflected in more than the cattle raids and feasts that took place within Celtic society. The Celts carried that warlike theme into many battles they fought against their enemies and were widely known for their bravery and prowess in war. As one modern historian phrases it, "The ferocity of their first assault inspired terror even in the ranks of veteran armies."[19] Among the battle tactics that earned Celtic soldiers that reputation were engaging in wild, screaming charges at their opponents; painting their bodies in bright colors; and sometimes fighting naked to further disconcert the enemy.

In fact, the soldiers in the first Roman army ever to face a Celtic one were a good deal more than disconcerted. In 390 B.C., not long after a large group of Gallic Celts (that is, Celts from Gaul) had migrated into northern Italy, a Gallic army marched southward, sacking one town after another along the way. When it finally threatened Rome, the city's leaders hastily called up the local militia. On July 18 a force of Roman troops

Celts were widely known for their bravery in warfare.

An Unlucky Date

The defeat at Allia was more than just embarrassing for the Romans. They came to believe that evil forces had been at work. Therefore, July 18 became known as the dark "Day of Allia" on Rome's calendar, an unlucky date on which to avoid doing business and other important activities.

numbering perhaps thirty thousand confronted a large mass of Gauls at the Allia River (a few miles north of Rome).

Unfortunately for Rome, a majority of its soldiers that day were new recruits. As the first-century-A.D. Greek writer Plutarch said, "Most of them were raw soldiers, and as such had never handled a weapon before."[20] These young troops fearfully beheld the great throng of enemy fighters—some wearing animal skins, the others nearly naked, and all decked out in war paint.

Suddenly, the Gauls broke into a riotous charge, shouting shrill cries as they went. This display of unbridled ferocity proved too much for the Roman recruits, who turned and ran for their lives. That left their more experienced comrades in the lurch, and they soon fled as well, turning the engagement into an easy victory for the Celtic marauders. (This defeat motivated the Romans to overhaul their military, which subsequently became the finest fighting machine in the known world and more than a match for Celtic armies.)

Parallel Worlds

The young Romans who shamed themselves that day had no idea what had inspired their fearsome attackers. No one outside the Celtic lands yet knew about Cuchulain and the other colorful but formidable super-warriors of the Celtic myths. Many of the Gauls who fought that day likely modeled their looks and behavior on those of Conall Cermach, Cuchulain, and other legendary heroes.

What is more, most Celtic warriors did not fear death. They believed that if they died in battle, they would join the gods and heroes in a hidden but very real Otherworld. This shows clearly the remarkable extent to which the Celts' mythic world affected what they thought and did in the parallel sphere of their everyday lives.

CHAPTER 2

Tales of the Celtic Cosmos and Gods

Celtic mythology consists of a collection of curious and compelling memories. To the ancient Celts they fondly recalled a bygone, very special world that was filled with colors almost too beautiful to perceive and sounds nearly too delightful to imagine. It was a place inhabited by human-like gods and godlike humans. They walked or rode through lush, lime-green forests and flower-covered meadows crisscrossed by chilly, sparkling streams. There were also rolling hills, atop which massive, brooding fortresses towered over the valleys below.

The dwellers on those heights, most often gods with names hard for ordinary humans to pronounce, kept silent watch over the weird and wonderful Otherworld they ruled. Its marvels are now seen only in storybooks. They included fairies and monsters, witches and ghosts, beautiful maidens who needed rescuing, and handsome heroes who performed seemingly impossible feats to accomplish those rescues.

The Celts believed that the deities who ruled that extraordinary cosmos, or universe, were most often wise and very powerful. But they were not quite strong enough to resist the onrush of the realm of men. Human civilization surrounded and eventually pushed aside the deities' once all-encompassing Otherworld.

As the great early twentieth-century Irish poet William Butler Yeats eloquently put it, the Celtic gods "are indeed more wise and beautiful than men. But men," in the end, "are stronger than they are. For men are, as it were, the foaming tide-line of their sea,"[21] that is, the barrier that encircles and threatens to engulf them. In this way, Yeats suggested, ordinary humans left the embrace of the old gods and went on to shape their own society and fate. Yet those divinities and other supernatural beings still inhabited their invisible cosmos. Indeed, the Celts firmly believed, the mysterious Otherworlds containing the gods continued to exist somewhere in the twilight zone between night and day, or between dreaming and waking.

Myths of Irish Beginnings

Among those once powerful Celtic gods and the myths associated with them, the oldest, most complete, and least tainted and distorted by later peoples and writers were those of the Irish Celts. This is partly because Ireland was the Celtic land whose culture was the last to be forever altered by contact with both the Greco-Roman and medieval European civilizations. Celtic culture had largely faded from much of Europe by A.D. 500 or 600. But it persisted to a considerable degree in Ireland for several more centuries, despite the increasing changes wrought by the arrival of Christianity there.

During those medieval centuries, Christian monks preserved many of the old Celtic myths—which had traditionally been passed on orally—by writing them down, often in poetic form. Several of these treatises have survived, providing an imperfect but invaluable sketch of these tales. By contrast, most similar documents from Celtic regions in continental Europe and elsewhere were either never written or lost over time.

Of these myths from Celtic Ireland, among the more important are those describing how that land was first populated. Many of these tales were recorded in *The Book of Invasions*, an eleventh-century work compiled by an anonymous Irish Christian, most likely a monk. According to that source, at first Ireland had no people and was dominated by a race of hideous sea monsters called the Fomorians.

During medieval times Christian monks wrote down many old Celtic myths in order to preserve them for posterity.

As time went on, the story goes, successive waves of gods and humans arrived in Ireland, and some of them fought the Fomorians for control of the island. Among these immigrants were the members of a race of human-like gods known as the Tuatha De Danann, or "followers of Dana (or Danu)," a powerful mother goddess. Among others, they included Brigid, goddess of healing; Aengus, deity of love; and Bodb Derg, god of wisdom and poetry. Supposedly these deities appeared from a hole in the sky and challenged the Fomorians. As University of Wales scholar Miranda J. Green tells it,

When the Tuatha occupied the land, the Fomorians caused them great trouble, pillaging their territory and imposing crippling taxes with dreadful punishments for defaulters. The Fomorians had an awesome leader,

Balor of the Baleful Eye, the gaze of whose single great eye caused instant death, and who could not be slain by any weapon [except for a blow to his eye].[22]

In a great battle, one of the Tuatha, Lugh, master of craftspeople, slew Balor with a sling shot through the eye. In this way the Tuatha gained control of Ireland. They were not fated to rule forever, however. Eventually, a large group of Celts called the Milesians landed on the island and in a series of battles defeated the Tuatha, who retreated underground into a hidden Otherworld. Many Celts believed that the Tuatha transformed themselves into fairies who continued to dwell in out-of-the-way places. One old Irish tradition claimed that some of these beings briefly entered the human world each year on Midsummer's Eve—June 21, the summer solstice.

Many Celts believed the gods known as the Tuatha De Danaan transformed themselves into fairies.

Myths Used for Political Gains

It is important to recall that these stories about the gods recounted in *The Book of Invasions* are Christian versions of earlier pagan myths. The originals no longer exist. So it is difficult to know which of the early Irish Celtic gods were most important and what roles they played in the cosmos and society.

The main problem is that the book's author sanitized, or cleaned up, the original pagan tales. He did this partly by removing pagan ideas and customs he felt were either anti-Christian or promoted pre-Christian religious ideas. He also added some concepts of his own, including the idea that the Milesians were the descendants of characters who were present in Egypt and the Middle East when the biblical Moses led the Hebrews out of Egypt. This gave the Milesians a connection to the Bible, and through it to early Christianity. His goal is now plain. He and other churchmen viewed the older Celtic deities and beliefs as misguided or corrupt, and he wanted to show that Christianity would inevitably triumph over them.

That writer was largely successful in achieving his goal. Over the ensuing centuries, various would-be kings and other rulers in Ireland used the myth of the Milesians to acquire political legitimacy. The argument was often that one's opponent was illegitimate because he was not a descendant of the original Celtic Milesians. As late as the 1630s, a noted Irish priest and writer publicly cited the myth of the Milesians. He claimed it proved that Charles I, king of England, Scotland, and Ireland from 1625 to 1649, was the legitimate ruler because the myth showed he was descended from early biblical people.

Bran's Legendary Voyage

The vestiges of Celtic culture that survived well into medieval times in Ireland also continued to create new myths, sometimes aided by local monks. These tales sometimes combined elements from older pagan myths with newer events and characters from the period immediately following Christianity's arrival on the island. A notable example

On his sea voyages, Bran sailed in vessels like this one, made of wood and ox hide and called a currach.

was the story of a journey to the legendary Land of Women. It seems to have initially been a pagan Otherworld centering on some remote Atlantic islands inhabited by enchanted goddesses.

The original version of the tale is lost. But a Christian version appears in *The Voyage of Bran*, penned around 700 in a monastery near Belfast, in northeastern Ireland. It is the oldest known example of an Irish literary form called *immram*, which tells about adventurous voyages to faraway, unknown islands.

In the story an Irish Celt named Bran mac Febal was walking on a beach and suddenly heard some beautiful music. He also saw an apple tree with white blossoms and carried some of the flowers home. No sooner had he entered his house when a strangely dressed woman appeared. She told him about the Land of Women, a faraway realm where neither decay nor death occurred. "There is nothing rough or harsh," the woman said, but only "sweet music striking on the ear, without grief, without sorrow, without death." It is "a beauty of a wondrous land."[23]

Desiring to find that alluring place, Bran launched three boats, each having a crew of nine. The vessels sailed westward for several days and suddenly received an unexpected visit from the Celtic sea god Manannan, who told them the place they sought was truly wondrous and urged them to keep going. They did so, and after a few more days they finally reached the Land of Women. Its strikingly beautiful queen welcomed them and invited them to stay in her palace. They found the place so comfortable that they lingered there for an entire year, but eventually they grew homesick and decided to depart.

As they neared the Irish coast, they saw a fishing boat and stopped to speak with its occupants. The conversation that ensued revealed an unexpected and shocking reality—namely, during the year the travelers had spent on the island, several centuries had elapsed in Ireland. So everyone that Bran and his companions knew had died long ago. Feeling that they no longer belonged in their

Mountain in the Sea

One of the most fascinating scenes in the myth of Bran and Branwen (see pages 42–45) is the one in which the enormous Bran and the ships carrying his Welsh army approach the Irish coast. This well-worded version of the scene is by the nineteenth-century Celtic mythologist Charles Squire.

No one in Ireland knew they [Bran and his soldiers] were coming until the royal swineherds, tending their pigs near the seashore, beheld a marvel. They saw a forest on the surface of the sea—a place where certainly no forest had been before—and, near it, a mountain with a lofty ridge on its top, and a lake on each side of the ridge. Both the forest and the mountain were swiftly moving toward Ireland. They informed Matholwch, who could not understand it, and sent messengers to ask Branwen what she thought it might be. "It is the men of the Island of the Mighty," said she, "who are coming here because they have heard of my ill-treatment. The forest that is seen on the sea is made of the masts of ships. The mountain is my brother Bran, wading into shoal water. The lofty ridge is his nose, and the two lakes, one on each side of it, are his eyes." The men of Ireland were terrified.

Charles Squire. *Celtic Myth and Legend.* Franklin Lakes, NJ: New Page, 2001, pp. 291–292.

native land, the travelers decided to sail on in hopes of finding a new home.

The three vessels mentioned in the myth were currachs, ancient craft made of wood and ox hide. The same kind of boats were frequently used by early medieval Irish monks, who made daring journeys in which they searched for unknown islands. There they hoped to create retreats where they might live quietly, meditate, and write. Groups of monks reached the Orkneys, off Scotland's northern coast, by 579; the Shetlands, a bit farther north, by 620; and Iceland by about 795.

Modern experts think there was a connection between these real voyages and the mythical one of Bran's. The question is which came first. Did the original pagan story inspire some of the early monks to embark on their own quests to find legendary islands? Or did the first of the monks' voyages become the basis for the Christian version of Bran's tale? No one knows for sure. But it is certain that Celtic myths remained powerful forces in people's lives in Ireland even after Christianity took root there.

Midir's Love for Étaín

The Voyage of Bran was only one of many legends of Celtic Otherworlds and primeval gods that captured the public imagination in medieval Ireland. Another was the love story of Midir and Étaín. A son of the Dagda, the father figure and leader of the Tuatha, Midir ruled part of a vast underground Otherworld. Étaín was a human Irish princess known for her great beauty.

The story begins when Midir laid eyes on Étaín for the first time. He was immediately captivated. Although he was already married to Fuamnach, a witch-goddess who knew how to cast spells, he wooed Étaín, and to his delight she returned his love.

The jealous Fuamnach could not accept her husband's relationship with Étaín, however. Fuming with anger,

Human Sacrifice

When the famous Roman military general Julius Caesar conquered Gaul (now France), he claimed that the Celtic natives practiced a form of human sacrifice. Modern experts think he was right. At least two thousand bodies of Celts killed in religious ceremonies have been found in peat bogs across Ireland and northern Europe.

the witch cast a terrible spell on Étaín to turn her into a fly and created a mighty wind that blew her far away. The unfortunate young woman eventually landed in the mansion of a local chieftain named Etar. A great feast was in progress, and Étaín fell into the drinking cup belonging to Etar's wife. Not noticing the tiny fly, the woman took a sip of wine and in the process swallowed Étaín. Instead of dying, however, Étaín miraculously survived as a seed in the woman's body and nine months later was born again as Etar's daughter. Moreover, for reasons no one can explain, the parents dubbed the child Étaín, the same name she had had before.

Meanwhile, as the new Étaín was growing up, Midir was frantically searching for the young woman he had come to love. Finally he found her, all grown up into a beautiful princess living in Etar's palace. But the young woman did not remember the prior relationship she had enjoyed with Midir, so he proceeded to describe it to her.

"What is it you are saying," she asked, "and who are you yourself?" "It is easy to tell that," he said. "I am Midir." "And what parted us if I was your wife?" asked Étaín. "It was through Fuamnach's sharp jealousy and through [her] spells [that] we were parted," he answered. "And you will come away with me now?"[24]

Sacral Kingship Brings Prosperity

At first, because she still could not remember the past, Étaín refused to leave with Midir. However, when he took her in his arms and kissed her on the lips, she suddenly recalled everything from her former life. At this point they made good their escape from the palace, aided by Midir's ability to transform both of them into animal form. As the late British mythologist Augusta Gregory told it, "All the armed men in the house made a rush at him then, but he rose up through the roof, bringing Étaín with him, and when they rushed out of the house to follow him, all they could see was two swans high up in the air, linked together by a chain of gold."[25]

To people today this myth seems to be little more than a charming folktale illustrating the power of the bond between devoted lovers. To the Irish Celts, however, it was much more

Midir and Étaín escape from Etar's mansion by rising into the air and exiting through the roof.

than that. For them there was a deeper, more broadly cultural meaning that related to the well-being, prosperity, and success of society as a whole. It was based on ancient beliefs about the benefits of a marriage between a deity and a king, princess, or other member of a royal family. "Irish myth," Green explains,

> contains the theme of sacral kingship, whereby the union of king and goddess promotes the prosperity of the land. Interestingly, the concept of divine love and marriage has a counterpart in the archaeological evidence for pagan Celtic religion. Divine couples . . . were venerated. In these cults, the partnership itself seems to be symbolically significant and to produce harmony and prosperity.[26]

Divine Beings in Human Form

The custom of sacral kingship was not limited to the Irish Celts, but rather recognized by many other Celtic peoples, including those in Wales. Similarly, the Welsh and other Celts also developed their own popular myths about the ancient gods and the singular cosmos they inhabited. Many of those surviving tales portray the deities as kings, queens, and other human-like beings who take part in most familiar human activities. According to scholar Peter B. Ellis, the reason for picturing the divine beings in this manner was that the Celts often perceived them as human ancestors rather than as the creators of the world. Most of those gods are "totally human," Ellis writes, and therefore "subject to all the natural virtues and vices. No sin is exempt from practice by the gods or humans."[27]

Another human-like attribute of most Celtic deities was that they were mortal, instead of immortal as most other ancient peoples' gods were portrayed. That is, the Celtic gods could be killed or die by accident. The main quality that set them apart in this respect was that if they did die, they came back, most often in some kind of spirit form. Thus, even though their bodies were not eternal, their spirits were.

Another superior quality enjoyed by the Celtic gods was various exceptional abilities; for instance, unusually great size, speed, strength, and/or intelligence. Also, some of these beings were expert magicians, poets, artists, and musicians. All of these superior abilities and skills earned them tremendous respect and admiration among the Celts, and the bulk of Celtic worship revolved around rituals intended to show that esteem. The details of most of those rites are no longer clear, but they probably included prayer, feasting, making offerings (sacrifices) of animals and plants, initiation ceremonies, and taking part in healing rites such as dunking the body in a pond or stream viewed as sacred. Some of these customs and the beliefs

Saint Brendan's Voyage

According to tradition, one of the Christian monks who sailed from Ireland in search of legendary islands was Brendan, later recognized as a saint. If real, his voyage took place sometime in the early A.D. 500s. The location of the island he supposedly found remains unknown.

behind them were pictured in various myths. Sacred bodies of water, for example, appear in a large number of ancient Celtic tales.

In contrast to the Druids, the early medieval monks who first wrote down the myths, some of whom were Celts themselves, worshipped the single Christian God. So they did not believe the traditional Celtic gods were divine. Nevertheless, some early Christians in Ireland and other Celtic lands did suspect those ancient deities might be real beings, reasoning that if so, they could be evil spirits or manifestations of the devil. Such beliefs naturally colored the monks' written versions of the old myths. It was not unusual, for example, for a churchman to transform a traditional god into an evil magician or the wicked relative of a story's hero.

Branwen's Unfortunate Marriage

This sort of recasting of gods in the roles of villains can be seen in one of the more familiar and beloved of the Welsh Celtic myths—the tale of Bran the Blessed. Bran is pictured as an immense human-like individual—a son of the Welsh sea god Llyr. Other important characters in the story include Llyr's daughter (and Bran's sister), Branwen; and Bran and Branwen's half-brother, Efnisien. It is Efnisien whom the author may have transformed into a scoundrel in the tale's Christian telling. Various modern scholars call the character antisocial, warped, mean spirited, and perverted.

As the story begins, the ancient lands of Wales and Ireland had been at war for a long time. Desiring peace, an Irish king, Matholwch, asked the Welsh princess Branwen to marry him. Hopefully, he reasoned, that would bring the two peoples together in friendship.

Branwen accepted the proposal, and many individuals on both sides, among them the enormous Bran, had high hopes for the upcoming union. One who did *not* approve of the marriage was the rude and often nasty Efnisien. To show his opposition, in the words of mythologist Arthur Cotterell, he slipped into the Irish king's camp and "cut off

Romano-Celtic Gods and Myths

The gods of the Celts who inhabited northern Europe and the British Isles remained largely unchanged until several of these areas had contact with Roman civilization. Notable examples were Rome's conquests of Gaul in the first century B.C. and Britain in the century that followed. The Romans introduced their own gods and myths to the Celts. But the religiously tolerant Romans also permitted most Celtic worship and myth telling to continue. Furthermore, the Romans welcomed a number of Celtic gods into their own belief system, in the process creating some hybrid Romano-Celtic deities. One was a war goddess named Andraste. Others included Aveta, a goddess of birth and midwifery, and Ocelus, a deity associated with healing.

Most of the myths of the Romano-Celtic gods have been lost. One that survived, however, is a tale about the ferocious Andraste. She became a leading deity of the Celtic Iceni tribe, which dwelled in eastern England. In A.D. 60 the Iceni queen Boudicca launched an insurrection against the Romans, and just prior to the first battle she invoked Andraste's support. In a speech to her soldiers, the warrior queen suggested that the war goddess, though invisible, happily stood among them. In the words of the Roman historian Dio Cassius, Boudicca "raised her hand toward heaven" and said, "I thank thee, Andraste, and call upon thee as woman speaking to woman." At this, the troops shouted their approval. The queen then added, "I supplicate [beg] and pray thee for victory, preservation of life, and liberty against men insolent, unjust, insatiable, impious."

Boudicca and her soldiers soon sacked two Roman cities. They strongly believed that Andraste had taken part in and thereby assured those victories. This newly created myth spread to other Celtic tribes that hated Rome, and it inspired them for years to come.

Dio Cassius. *Roman History.* Book 62. Translated by Ernest Cary. Brainfly.net. www.brainfly.net/html/books/diocas62.htm.

Boudicca's soldiers sack Londinium (London) in A.D. 60.

the lips, ears, and tails of Matholwch's horses during the wedding feast in Wales. Not unnaturally, hostilities almost broke out between the Irish and the Welsh as a result. But Bran managed to avoid a war by presenting Matholwch with a magic cauldron."[28]

Although receiving that gift calmed the king down, he remained angry about losing his much-loved horses. As time went on, therefore, he started taking out his frustration on his new wife. He demanded that she clean the palace and help the royal chef prepare meals, for example. Moreover, the

Branwen uses a starling to send a message to Bran about the cruelties of her husband, Matholwch.

king ordered the chef to box the queen's ears once each day just for spite.

Matholwch also made sure that no news of his ill treatment of Branwen got out, so Bran and her other relatives had no idea what was happening. Bran did eventually find out, however. Enraged, he quickly raised an army, which boarded ships and sailed for Ireland, while Bran himself, on account of his great size, waded through the water.

In the battle that followed, Bran and his forces were victorious and Matholwch was killed. But Bran was badly wounded, and it looked as if he might die. At that point he shocked everyone by ordering some of his soldiers to cut off his head and take it back to Wales. They should bury it, he said, after which it would become a magic charm that would stave off would-be invaders. The soldiers were in for another shock. After they sliced off Bran's head, it continued to look at and speak to them. Only when they buried it did its mouth stop talking.

Severed Heads

The Celtic preoccupation with severed heads extended to warfare. In addition to using war paint and fighting naked except for belts, some Celtic warriors tried to frighten their enemies by hanging human heads from those belts or from their chariots.

Grisly but Fascinating Reminders

Modern experts feel that this tale of Bran's rescue of his sister reveals much about ancient Celtic society. First, they say, it implies that Ireland and Wales had diplomatic contact, and perhaps social ties among royals as well, in ancient times. Archaeologists have indeed confirmed this. The two lands carried on trade with each other and at times established colonies on each other's soil. The war mentioned in the story may therefore be a garbled memory of actual combat caused by disputes over such colonies.

The tale also echoes some real ancient Celtic religious ideas about human heads. "It is important to remember that, for the ancient Celts, the soul reposed in the head," Ellis points out. Many Celts, he explains, kept "the heads of those people they respected, embalming them with cedar oil, and thus paying reverence to great souls. They were not, as some have claimed, head *hunters*. Only the heads of those already slain in battle, friend or foe, were taken as trophies, and always people worthy of respect."[29]

Sometimes the heads were stored in special areas protected by the Druids. People also deposited severed heads in sacred Celtic rivers or lakes as offerings to the gods who dwelled in or oversaw those waterways. Such images remain grisly but fascinating reminders of the numerous links between the Celts' own lives and the mythical cosmos inhabited by their gods.

CHAPTER 3

Memorable Mythical Celtic Heroes

The gods in their magical Otherworlds constituted only a small subdivision of the vast totality of Celtic mythology. The Celtic peoples of ancient and early medieval Europe were often even more enthralled with the stories of an impressive assembly of legendary human heroes. Each tribe or region had a favorite champion and eagerly perpetuated tales about him. Unfortunately for posterity, accounts of many of these mythical characters disappeared over the centuries, so their identities and stories are lost to human memory.

Still, tales about some of the beloved Celtic superheroes *have* survived. This was especially the case in the folklore of Ireland, Wales, and a few other areas in which remnants of ancient Celtic culture persisted into the medieval era. The exploits of handsome, fearsome heroes like Cuchulain, Finn McCool, and Culhwch continued to be told and retold, at first by word of mouth and later in written narratives.

Their bravery, military skills, sense of justice, and sheer vitality were not simply literary and mythical inventions. Rather, the qualities that made them tick were reflections of the character and lives of those who created and over time added to their widely popular legends. Indeed, prominent scholar Christopher R. Fee points out, such heroes were, "in effect, Everyman," or the average Celt. In his or her own small way, that person aspired to display some of the same strength, courage, and ideals exhibited by the mythic heroes. Thus, says Fee, the hero's "trials, tribulations, battles, and journeys of growth and transformation mirrored [the ordinary individual's] own innermost fears, desires, and needs."[30]

Culhwch's Love Spell

To a large extent, this explains why the Welsh Celts had so much admiration for a daring, gallant knight named Culhwch. Although he performed numerous fearless feats, he was best known for his quest to find a beautiful young woman named Olwen. The son of an ancient Welsh ruler, King Cilydd, Culhwch never got to know his mother very well because she died when he was a boy. It was not long before Cilydd married again, giving Culhwch a stepmother.

Almost from the beginning, Culhwch did not get along with the new queen. So when he grew into a young man and she recommended that he marry her daughter, his stepsister, he showed no interest. "I am not yet of an age to wed,"[31] he told her a bit too politely.

The stepmother did not take this refusal well. Her husband and stepson did not know that she was a witch who had the power to cast spells on people, and this she now did to Culhwch. She implanted in his mind the idea that the only woman he could ever love or marry was Olwen, the beautiful daughter of a huge and hideous ogre named Ysbaddaden.

Under the influence of the love spell, Culhwch thought of nearly nothing else but finding and marrying Olwen, a person he had never met. The problem, the sympathetic Cilydd told his son, was that the giant, one-eyed Ysbaddaden despised strangers and kept his daughter securely hidden behind the towering walls of his impregnable castle. Perhaps, the king suggested, Culhwch's powerful cousin, Arthur, a king who commanded several stalwart knights, might be able to help the youth get access to Olwen.

The Ogre and the Maiden

Sure enough, hearing of the young man's plight, Arthur sent three of his knights along with Culhwch to the giant's castle.

Culhwch, with Olwen, asks her father, the ogre Ysbaddaden, for Olwen's hand in marriage. The giant gave Culhwch a set of seemingly impossible tasks to perform first.

The knights searched the area diligently and finally found a local herdsman's wife who knew Olwen. The wife agreed to take Olwen a message. It requested that the young woman slip out of her father's castle after nightfall and secretly meet with Culhwch. That evening Culhwch saw someone approaching the meeting place, and his heart skipped a beat when he realized it was the woman he was madly in love with. According to Richard Barber, who specializes in medieval literature, "The girl was clothed in a robe of flame-colored silk. Round her neck was a collar of red gold, on which were precious emeralds and rubies. Her hair was more yellow than the flower of the

Magic Cauldrons

The cauldron that Bran gave to the king to pacify him supposedly had magical properties. In particular, if one placed a dead warrior inside, he would be restored to life. Other cauldrons in Celtic mythology were said to contain vast stores of wisdom or liquids with potent healing powers.

broom [bush], and her skin was whiter than the foam of the wave, and her hands and fingers were fairer than [blossoms, and] her glance was brighter than the eye of the trained hawk."[32]

The meeting was eventful, for it took less than a minute for the maiden to be smitten with love for Culhwch. Before they parted, she gave him the following advice: "Go and ask my father for my hand and agree to do whatever he shall require of you, and you will get me. But if you refuse anything, you will *not* get me."[33]

Culhwch did as Olwen urged. He gained an audience with Ysbaddaden and firmly requested the hand of his daughter in marriage. But the monstrous ogre made it clear that there was no way he would agree to the request unless the young suitor accomplished each task on a long list. The chores were extremely difficult, including dismantling a small mountain and planting crops in a vast field, both in the same day. If and when Culhwch could complete all the assignments on the list, Ysbaddaden snorted, then and only then could there be a discussion about a marriage.

The giant seemed confident that the young visitor had no chance of meeting the demands. But Ysbaddaden was in for a major surprise. After a few weeks Culhwch returned to the castle and announced that he had fulfilled all the ogre's requirements. Then it was the young hero's turn to be surprised. Ysbaddaden indicated that he was not going to keep his end of the bargain and allow his daughter to marry. At this, Culhwch grew angry and killed the giant, and not long afterward he and Olwen became husband and wife.

The Ferocious, Sacred Boar

At first glance, the story of Culhwch and Olwen may seem to be little more than a pleasant fantasy that mixes the romantic themes of love, witchcraft, and heroic quests. Yet as is true of many other myths, it also reflects some actual Celtic social customs—though clearly in exaggerated form. In the story, for example, the most difficult and dangerous of all the tasks Ysbaddaden gave Culhwch was to hunt down a huge wild boar and pull out its tusks. It so happens that numerous other Celtic myths contain episodes in which men must hunt and kill wild boars as rites of passage or tests of courage.

Similarly, in many real-life Celtic tribes a prospective husband was asked to perform some sort of daring or difficult feat in order to earn the right to ask for a woman's hand in marriage. Most often that feat entailed hunting and slaying a dangerous wild beast. It might be a wolf or a bear, but usually, as in the myths, it was a boar. In large part this was because that powerful, feisty creature was thought to personify war and the warrior's spirit. "The wild boar was a symbol of ferocity, both physically and visually," researcher David James explains. "And the Celts believed that its spirit

A Celtic bronze boar from the first century A.D. The boar was sacred in Celtic culture and appears in many folktales.

Celtic Marriages

Information about ancient Celtic marriage has been pieced together from isolated remarks made in surviving ancient literary sources and some widely scattered archaeological finds. So the exact nature of the Celts' marriage customs remains somewhat uncertain. Further complicating and confusing the issue is the fact that these customs may have differed in various ways among the many and often widely spaced Celtic tribes and regions. Nevertheless, most of these societies seem to have shared a few basic ideas about marriage. First, large numbers of marriages were arranged by relatives well before the prospective bride and groom were of marriageable age. Yet it appears that in many Celtic lands, women had most of the same civil rights as men and could not be forced to marry against their will. Thus, when a girl came of age she could agree to the arrangement or not, and if not, presumably the original deal was nullified. One of the major purposes of Celtic marriage, as is true in Western countries today, was the protection of children. Celtic marriages also protected the property rights of the husband and male children and in some tribes those of the mothers and female children as well. In cases in which the father, mother, or both owned property before the wedding, they often signed prenuptial agreements (contracts ensuring that in case of divorce one party could not take the other's property). If neither spouse owned any property, no formal agreement regarding property rights was necessary. In addition, it appears that some Celtic groups allowed trial marriages that last lasted a year or so. They had no binding contracts; so long as no children were involved, the parties could go their separate ways with no questions asked at the end of the trial period.

would make their warriors fierce in battle. As well as helmets with boar sculptures on them, some fine free-standing sculptures of the boar have been found"[34] in the tombs of Celtic warriors.

In addition, in some Celtic regions boars were considered sacred. In part this was because it was thought that they originated in the Otherworld in which the gods dwelled. Also, various deities were said to have the ability to shape-shift into the form of a boar. Deep respect for the boar is seen throughout Celtic mythology, including one of the myths involving the healing goddess Brigid. In that tale a boar wanders into one of her sacred compounds, and instead of killing it she allows it to live out the rest of its life there.

The Irish Achilles

In spite of his valor and resolve, as a character Culhwch never attained the enormous stature that another mythic hero, Cuchulain, did. Because very few original mythological accounts have survived from the European continental Celtic societies, it is uncertain whether they held him or equivalent legendary characters in high esteem. It is certain, however, that he was the Irish Celts' greatest national hero.

Hailing from Ulster, then covering much of northern Ireland, Cuchulain is often referred to as the "Irish Achilles," a reference to the heroic main character in the ancient Greek poet Homer's renowned epic the *Iliad*. Like Achilles, Cuchulain had a short but glorious existence. Both heroes felt that it was better to die young and achieve everlasting fame than to live a long but commonplace life. "If I stay here and fight," Homer had Achilles say, death would soon come. True, "there would be no homecoming for me." Yet "my fame will never die!"[35] Echoing these words were those of Cuchulain, who declared, "I care not if I last but a day, if my name and my fame are a power forever."[36]

Cuchulain's original birth name was Setanta, given to him by his mother, Dechtire, daughter of one of Ulster's high priests. The identity of his father is somewhat uncertain. Some ancient sources say he was a mortal man, while others claim the Celtic deity Lugh was Setanta's father.

Whoever his father was, when only five years old Setanta was already stronger and no less ambitious than an adult man. Wasting no time, the boy traveled to Ulster's capital, Emain Macha, and confronted the king, Conchobhar. Impressed by Setanta's physical prowess and sheer boldness, Conchobhar allowed him to stay in Emain Macha and train to become a warrior. In truth Ulster badly needed as many skilled fighters as could be found to defend it against attacks by Connaught, the kingdom lying to its south.

A New Name

Conchobhar soon came to see that he had made the right decision in sponsoring young Setanta. When the boy was seven, Ulster's widely respected blacksmith, Culain (or Culann), threw a party for the king. Forgetting that Setanta had been invited but had not yet arrived, after the other guests were assembled Culain placed his huge, ferocious guard dog outside the gate to his house. A few minutes later Setanta approached the gate, and the dog immediately attacked him. The boy "had no weapon but his stick and his ball," as Augusta Gregory told it. "But when he saw the hound coming at him, he [threw] the ball with such force that it went down his throat and through his body. Then he seized him by the hind legs and dashed him against a rock until there was no life left in him."[37]

Conchobhar and the other guests were astounded at the boy's feat of bravery and strength. But Culain was quite naturally upset over the loss of his dog. Gently, Setanta took the man's hand, apologized, and offered to take the hound's place as a guard until the blacksmith had trained another dog. Culain agreed, and from then on Setanta was known as Cuchulain, meaning "the hound of Culain."

In the years that followed, Cuchulain performed one feat of strength and valor after another, in so doing becoming the greatest fighting champion that Ulster, and all of Ireland, had ever seen. People were in awe of him not only because of his courage and skills as a warrior. They also respected him because he seemed to possess numerous magical powers.

When Cuchulain was seventeen, he faced a challenge that many feared he would not be able to overcome. The queen of Connaught, Medb, amassed the biggest army the Irish had ever witnessed and marched it toward Ulster. At the time, a magical curse concocted by an angry goddess kept the rest of Ulster's soldiers immobilized and unable to fight. So Cuchulain sprang into action and by himself kept the enemy troops at bay, slaying hundreds of them each day.

Unfortunately for Ulster's mighty hero, however, he was wounded several times during each attack. So he grew a bit weaker each day. Finally, Cuchulain was unable to stop the onrushing enemy by himself. By virtue of their greater numbers, the soldiers of Connaught managed to kill him. Yet only a few minutes later, Ulster's warriors broke free of the curse, rushed onto the battlefield, and decisively defeated the invaders. By buying needed time, therefore, Cuchulain had saved Ulster from destruction.

When Setanta took the place of Culain's ferocious hound, he received a new name, Cuchulain, meaning "the hound of Culain."

Immersed in Magic

The Celts of ancient and medieval Ireland thrilled at hearing recitations of these and several other heroic deeds performed by Cuchulain. This was partly because the tales of kings, royal courts, battles, intrigue, and superhuman feats associated with him were fun for listeners. In an age with few or no books and no radio, TV, movies, or other media, tales about the hero provided occasional, much-needed relief from the drudgery and monotony of everyday life.

More importantly, the myths that starred the mighty Cuchulain strongly appealed to the Irish people's sense of nationalism, or deep feelings of patriotism for their nation. Initially, as expected, the stories inspired such feelings mainly among the residents of Ulster. Over time, however, they spread all over Ireland. Moreover, Cuchulain's exploits continued to arouse nationalistic feelings in modern times. In the early twentieth century, when Irish rebels fought to gain independence from Britain, popular writers among them helped the cause by calling on their fellow countrymen to remember the ancient hero and his deeds. There was an enormous response. Even though they knew that Cuchulain was a mythical figure, thousands of Irish rebels were inspired by him because he was said to have fought and died for the same thing they were fighting for—Irish freedom.

In contrast, the ancient and medieval Irish Celts viewed Cuchulain as a real figure from their past. They were drawn to him because he possessed a set of special qualities and skills that they related to on a fundamental level. First, he had a potent ability to employ magic and interact with supernatural powers. The Celts believed those powers had long existed all around them, in both mystical Otherworlds and the world of humans.

In that real world most Celts readily accepted the reality of magic charms, often worn around the neck. They also believed in magic potions that made those who drank them do things

Druids harvest mistletoe growing on an oak tree. Druids were believed to have had the ability to control storms and other natural forces.

they normally would not; the ability of some people to shape-shift into various animals; and reincarnation, a deceased person's return to life in another body. Other common beliefs held in at least some Celtic regions were that the human soul could reside within animals and that Druids and sorceresses had the ability to control storms and other natural forces.

An Otherworldly Beast

In addition to Cuchulain's ties to magic and the supernatural, the widespread belief that he was the son of the deity Lugh suggested that the young hero was himself part god. Also, whatever magical powers Cuchulain had inherited from his divine father had been enhanced by the boy's education. This was because one of his teachers had supposedly been a sorceress or prophetess. Furthermore, it was said that he wielded magical weapons, wore armor that could not be pierced by normal weapons, and could, with the aid of his charioteer, render his chariot invisible. Still another of Cuchulain's supernatural connections was the number 7, which Celtic society viewed as the most magical and powerful number. According to the legends, he had seven fingers on each hand, seven toes on each foot, and seven pupils in each eye.

Even more amazing was the unique and frightening transformation the young man experienced as he went into battle. It has been called by various names over the centuries, among them the "battle frenzy," the "killing trance," and the "warp spasm." As described in a medieval document that recounts one of Cuchulain's primary myths, *The Cattle Raid of Cooley*, a warp spasm

> made him into a monstrous thing, hideous and shape-less, unheard of. His shanks [limbs] and his joints, every knuckle and angle and organ from head to foot, shook like a tree in the flood or a reed in a stream. His body made a furious twist inside his skin, so that his feet and shins and knees twitched to the rear and his heels and calves switched to the front [and] he sucked one eye [deep] into his head [and] the other eye fell out along his cheek. His mouth weirdly distorted [and] his lungs and liver flapped in his mouth and throat. . . . Malignant mists and spurts of fire [appeared above] his

head, so fierce was his fury, [and from his head burst a] spout of black blood darkly and magically smoking.[38]

Some modern writers have compared this incredible physical conversion with the one in which a mild-mannered man becomes the raging, violent Incredible Hulk, a popular character in modern comic books and movies. Needless to say, many of Cuchulain's enemies took one look at the otherworldly beast he had become and ran for their lives. It is no wonder that the Irish Celts, who were immersed in a mystical, magical belief system, felt that his uncanny abilities and physical traits reflected a cherished facet of their culture.

The Gift of Knowledge

The ancient and medieval Irish were no less enamored of another remarkable mythical hero named Fionn mac Cumhaill, which translates into modern English as Finn McCool (or MacCool). According to most existing Irish lore, he was born sometime in the A.D. 200s. But scholars think the original character and some of his tales may have originated considerably earlier. Named Demne at birth, he later took the name Finn, meaning "fair," because his skin was unusually pale.

Fondly remembered for his bravery and generosity, Finn McCool is most famous for leading a band of intrepid young warrior-hunters known as the *fiana* (or Fenians). Their adventures took them across most of Ireland and even partway into Scotland. Each was extremely well educated and excelled as a tracker, hunter, warrior, and poet. The group sometimes fought for the Irish king Cormac mac Airt. But its members most often defended Ireland against attacks by armies of Vikings (or Norse), formidable raiders from nearby Scandinavia. The *fiana* occasionally battled serpents, giants, trolls, and wild boars as well. All of those exploits are described in the Fenian (or Fionn) Cycle. Also referred to as *fiana* lore, it is a body of legendary tales and poems about Finn and his companions.

Fingal's Cave

In Scotland, Finn was called Fingal. Tradition held that he and his followers maintained a base from which to fight the Vikings inside a cave on the Scottish island of Staffa. This legend inspired the nineteenth-century composer Felix Mendelssohn to write the atmospheric musical piece *Fingal's Cave*.

Finn's Son

According to legend, Finn McCool was married several times. Just as he could change himself into a deer, one of his mates had the ability to shape-shift into a doe. Just before she gave birth, she was told that if she licked her human baby, it would become and remain a deer; whereas if she refrained from licking it, it would remain human. She managed not to lick the infant. But at one point her tongue very slightly touched its forehead.

So the boy, whom they named Oisin, meaning "little fawn," thereafter had a small tuft of deer fur on his forehead.

The young man grew up to be a talented poet. He was also an effective warrior and traveled from time to time with his father and the other *fiana* on their adventures. But one day Oisin decided to leave his homeland, and for many years he rested quietly in one of the Otherworlds said to lie in the mysterious place where the sun sets each day. It was not until after Finn died that the son returned to Ireland. There he wandered from place to place until one day he met the now famous British Christian missionary Patrick. The two got to know each other, the story goes. Oisin told Patrick about Finn and the *fiana*, the heroic Cuchulain, the divine Tuatha, and the rest of the gods and heroes mentioned in the Irish myths. Realizing that Patrick's introduction of the Christian faith to Ireland would change that land forever, Oisin decided to depart. He returned to the Otherworld he had visited before and has supposedly remained there, hidden to human eyes, ever since.

Oisin told Patrick of the adventures of Finn McCool and the fiana.

One of the quainter tales about Finn tells how he acquired one of his finest personal gifts. When he was a boy, his mother hired a tutor for him, and that person—a mysterious Druid named Finegas—seems to have had special insights into the nature of the cosmos. Finegas taught Finn to catch and cook a unique fish called the Salmon of Knowledge and warned him not to eat it. After cooking it, however, the boy accidentally touched the salmon, burning his thumb in the process. Instinctively, he licked the thumb and thereby acquired a tremendous amount of knowledge. After that, Finn could produce answers to almost any question by chewing on his thumb.

This brief myth had an impact on the way medieval Celts regarded their diets. Because Finn supposedly gained much knowledge by touching a fish (and would have gained even more by eating it), the Irish came to call fish "brain food." That expression passed from generation to generation throughout the rest of medieval and early modern times and remains common today in English-speaking countries, including the United States.

A Man of Honor

Finn's abilities were not limited to the vast storehouse of information in his head, however. In some of his myths he was also a skilled shape-shifter. It was said that he could

An Extremely Difficult Initiation

According to one of the many myths about the fiana, *from time to time they took new members into their adventurous company. But they refused to accept anyone without extraordinary courage, strength, and endurance, and the extreme difficulty of their initiation rites reflected these very strict requirements. According to the late, great Irish scholar Proinsias Mac Cana, a would-be member*

Was armed with a shield and a hazel stick and placed standing up to his waist in a hole in the ground, and nine warriors cast their spears at him simultaneously. If he suffered from hurt thereby, he was not accepted into the group. Next, his hair was braided and he was made to run through the woods of Ireland pursued at a brief interval by all the warriors. If he was overtaken and wounded, he was not accepted. Moreover, if his weapons had quivered in his hand, if his hair had been disturbed by a hanging branch, or if a dead branch had cracked under his foot, then neither was he accepted.

Proinsias Mac Cana. *Celtic Mythology.* New York: Peter Bedrick, 1987, p. 105.

change himself into various animals, among them deer and boars. But his favorite disguise was that of a dog. This talent came in handy when he and the other *fiana* were hunting, as Finn could pretend to be a deer and thereby lure real deer out into the open.

The frequently long-range hunts in which the young warriors engaged carried them far and wide through both familiar human regions and the magical forests of uncanny Otherworlds. The late Irish scholar Proinsias Mac Cana remarked on

> the ease with which they pass from the natural world to the supernatural. Time after time they find themselves in pursuit of a magic stag or boar which leads them to a secluded dwelling where they encounter strange beings and undergo equally strange and often perilous experiences. In other ways too, they maintain constant dialogue with the people of the *sidh*, or subterranean Otherworld.[39]

The Giant's Causeway in Ireland. Legend says it was built by Finn McCool so he could cross the Irish Sea to Britain to fight the Scots.

It was the real world of humans in which Finn and his fellow champions left their greatest mark. In each successive generation of Irish Celts, most people believed that those heroes had lived less than a century before them. Moreover, it was thought that their most important achievement was to make Ireland safe from foreign intruders. The Irish "have always held," the nineteenth-century mythologist Charles Squire wrote, "that the Fenians were a kind of native militia, and that Finn was their general."[40]

The *fiana*, the medieval Irish felt, also set a kind of ethical standard for righteous folk in everyday life. As Squire wrote, Finn once promised "never to refuse hospitality to anyone who asked, never to turn his back in battle, and never to insult any woman."[41] In early Ireland nearly every parent, warrior, and ruler hoped he or she could contribute to society's greater good by being like Finn, a true man of honor.

CHAPTER 4

Early Arthurian Characters and Tales

Besides the tales of the gods and ancient Irish heroes, another major subdivision of Celtic mythology consists of stories about one of the world's most famous and beloved mythical individuals. Almost everyone is familiar with the full-blown legends of King Arthur. In those entertaining tales he was a medieval English ruler who governed a kingdom called Camelot from a grand, towering castle of the same name.

That resplendent residence contained the renowned Round Table, at which Arthur and his equally famous knights sat. Today several of them are household names, including Lancelot, Galahad, Gawain, and Percival. Also prominent in today's familiar cast of Arthurian characters are Camelot's lovely queen, Guinevere; Arthur's mysterious tutor, the magician Merlin; the king's resentful son, Mordred, who ended up turning on him; and the Lady of the Lake, the enigmatic nature deity who provided Arthur with his formidable sword, Excalibur.

Most of the classic Arthurian stories were based on a group of late medieval sources. They include Englishman Geoffrey of Monmouth's *History of the Kings of Britain* (circa 1136); various French, German, and English romances (romantic tales), notably five by the twelfth-century French

King Arthur's story has been told many times by many authors. This illustration is from Sir Thomas Mallory's Le Morte d'Arthur (The Death of Arthur) *in 1485.*

poet Chrétien de Troyes; and *Le Morte d'Arthur* (*The Death of Arthur*, 1485), a long romance by England's Thomas Mallory. All of these writers and their works were part of Europe's post-Celtic medieval society and culture. So it is not surprising that they pictured Arthur as a medieval English ruler.

Yet several of the authors in question based their Arthurian stories on earlier Celtic versions, most of which are lost. Of the few surviving old Celtic myths that served as a basis for the classic Arthurian tales, those from Wales are the most crucial. Among them is the tale of the hero Culhwch and his quest for the fair Olwen, in which Arthur and his knights play small but key roles. Today such early Welsh stories about Arthur are known mainly to literary scholars and a few hardcore Arthur enthusiasts. Yet though obscure, it is possible that without them Arthur may never have developed into one of the greatest literary figures of all time.

A Storybook Realm

Most of these very early Celtic Arthurian tales are part of a collection of Welsh myths known as the *Mabinogion*. It dates from sometime between A.D. 1000 and 1100. Yet the unknown authors clearly based the stories on much older Welsh legends. Geoffrey Ashe, one of the world's leading Arthurian scholars, says, "The events are supposed to happen a long time ago, but are really dateless." Moreover, he adds, "These linked tales are a literary creation using elements extending over a long stretch of time." Only one thing can be said with any certainty, Ashe says. It is that the tales are rooted "in Celtic antiquity,"[42] that is, back when the Celts were fighting the Romans or even earlier.

The ancient setting of these myths can readily be seen in the myth of Culhwch and Olwen. The main character's father, King Cilydd, is clearly a Celtic ruler whose kingdom coexists with and perhaps lies near Arthur's. The Romans are not mentioned. But the story's events could easily be set in the period in which they were in Britain. In such a case the section of Britain controlled by Rome would lie somewhere to the east of Cilydd's and Arthur's Celtic domains. Thus, Culhwch's myth could be alternately set in pre-Roman Britain (before A.D. 43) or in Roman Britain (from A.D. 43 to 410). Either way, the events of this story, and presumably the other tales told in the *Mabinogion*, are depicted as happening before the fall of Rome and start of medieval times (in the late 400s).

In whatever time period the tales are set, there is no doubt that they depict a storybook realm in which the seemingly impossible is often possible. "We are in a world where the marvelous is normal," Richard Barber writes, "and where the laws of everyday life are suspended. The figures who inhabit this world are shape-shifters, possessors of strange skills, and are certainly the heirs of the ancient gods, if not the gods themselves."[43]

God of Youthfulness

The term *Mabinogion*, employed in the title of a collection of medieval Welsh myths, seems to have been based on the name of a Celtic god called Mabon in Wales and Maponus in England. Associated with youthfulness, that deity was somewhat equivalent to the Greco-Roman god Apollo.

Shelter from the Storm

Among the "strange skills" Barber mentions is prophecy, or foretelling future events. Various ancient gods supposedly possessed that ability, along with a few unusually gifted humans. Among the latter in the Arthurian myths was the magician Merlin, who became Arthur's mentor. In Celtic tradition he was a Druid who foretold that the adult Arthur would help the native Celtic Britons defeat invaders from continental Europe.

A similar mystical skill that worked in a manner opposite to that of prophecy was the ability to revisit the past. In the Celtic myths, as in most other national mythologies, a person who witnesses either the past or future often does so in a dream. This occurs in one of the more mysterious myths from the *Mabinogion*, titled *The Dream of Rhonabwy*. It consists of a frame story, a literary form fairly common in mythologies around the globe. A typical frame story starts out in a certain place and time, and as the plot unfolds it switches—via a character's recollection or dream—to a different setting. Then, near the end, it returns to the original setting. In this case the main character, who lives centuries after Arthur's era, has a dream in which he is transported back to Arthur's world and then forward again to his own.

That main character, Rhonabwy, and his two companions were knights, retainers to a twelfth-century Welsh king named Madog. That ruler sent the three men to find and arrest his brother, Iorwerth, who had rebelled against the throne. The three knights searched for several days with no luck. Then, as the popular modern teller of the *Mabinogion* tales, the late Charlotte E. Guest, wrote, quite suddenly "there arose a storm of wind and rain, so that it was hardly possible to go forth with safety."[44] Fortunately for them, the men came upon a small house that sheltered them from the storm.

However, Rhonabwy and the others quickly found that their new situation was far from ideal. The house's owner, a

An Old Manuscript's Long Journey

The old books making up the original Welsh manuscript of the *Mabinogion* passed from family to family between about 1400 and 1701, until they landed in the library at Jesus College in Oxford, England. A bit more than a century later, Lady Charlotte Guest used them to create the first published English translation.

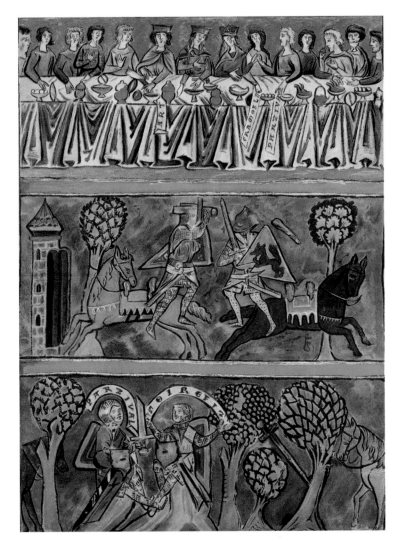

hermit named Heilyn, did not like having to share his food with them and treated them in a rude manner. Also, his home was downright filthy and crawling with bugs. Still, the visitors decided they must make the best of things, so without complaint they ate the paltry, tasteless dinner their host supplied. Next, in Guest's words,

> being weary from their journey, they laid themselves down and sought to sleep. And when they looked at the couch, it seemed to be made but of a little coarse straw full of dust and vermin . . . and after much

In a scene from "The Dream of Rhonabwy" from the Mabinogion, *King Arthur and Owain play chess while Arthur's men battle Owain's army of birds.*

suffering from the vermin, and from the discomfort of their couch, a heavy sleep fell on Rhonabwy's companions. But Rhonabwy, not being able either to sleep or to rest, thought he should suffer less if he went to lie upon the yellow calf-skin that was stretched out on the floor. And there he slept.[45]

A Peculiar Chess Game

Having fallen asleep, Rhonabwy experienced a highly realistic and vivid dream. He recognized the countryside he was in as the same section of eastern Wales and western England that he had known all his life. But there was something slightly different about it. Then in the distance he spied a structure he had never seen before—a massive, soaring castle, its beautifully decorated walls gleaming in the bright sunlight.

From that same direction, a well-dressed horseman approached Rhonabwy, dismounted, and introduced himself. His name was Iddawc, and he claimed to be a messenger of the mighty Arthur. Yonder castle, Iddawc said, was the legendary Camelot, the seat of Arthur's fair kingdom. When the surprised Rhonabwy identified himself, the other man offered to take him to meet the king. Iddawc explained that Arthur was gathering knights and other fighters with which to confront an army of invaders at nearby Mount Badon.

Not long afterward, the two men reached a large military camp surrounding a ford, or shallow spot, in a wide stream. "For a mile around the ford on both sides of the road, they saw tents and encampments, and there was the clamor of a

Did the Real Arthur Have a Court?

"Who was King Arthur and what was his court like?" asks researcher of Arthurian lore Gjoll Hobkynsson. Arthur was likely a fifth-century-A.D. military leader, Hobkynsson asserts, of "Romano-British" descent. By this, he means Roman-Celtic descent, as most of the Britons who lived in the fifth century, when Rome abandoned Britain, were—at least culturally speaking—Celts, Romans, or a mix of the two peoples. It is probable that the real Arthur was not a king, Hobkynsson admits, so it is doubtful he had a formal royal court. Yet what later legends called his court may have been an exaggerated memory of his following of high-ranking local military officers, who became his knights in the myths. The difficulty in describing Arthur and that following, Hobkynsson writes, is that

We are dealing with a cross over point between historical fact and myth. Around the time of King Arthur, Britain was suffering after the Romans had pulled out . . . in 410 A.D. The Britons had lived under the umbrella of the Roman Empire for over four centuries. In the southeast of the country there were many Empire citizens with a mixture of Roman and Romano-British blood. . . . [It is] likely that Arthur's [following of loyal, knight-like warriors] was heavily influenced by Roman civilization. This would have included the growing Christian faith. Arthur may have marked some sort of transition period between Celtic paganism and Christianity. Certainly kingship rites still had pagan elements in their symbolism. His queen [Guinevere] retires to become a nun at the end of the Arthurian cycle [of myths]. Thus the sovereignty of Britain as symbolised by Arthur's marriage to the land and the Queen, has become part of the Christian church.

Gjoll Hobkynsson. "The Celts and Saxons: A Barbarian Conspiracy." Druid Grove, the Order of Bards, Ovates & Druids. www.druidry.org/library/miscellaneous/celts-and-saxons-barbarian-conspiracy.

mighty host," as Guest described it. "And they came to the edge of the ford, and there they beheld Arthur sitting on a flat island below the ford." The king, wearing his shining battle armor, was surrounded by knights and churchmen. Iddawc, followed by the awed Rhonabwy, "stood before Arthur and saluted him."[46]

Arthur heartily greeted Iddawc and his companion. The king offered both men refreshments and a comfortable place to rest and then turned to one of his most trusted knights, Sir Owain. Arthur asked Owain if he would care to play chess; the knight said yes, and Rhonabwy watched with interest as they began to play.

Suddenly, another messenger rushed up to the king and announced that Arthur's squires, the young assistants to his knights, had attacked a flock of pet birds belonging to Owain. Hearing this, the anxious Owain requested that Arthur call off his squires. But the king responded only by telling Owain he should make his next move in the chess game. The messenger returned twice more with the same distressing news, and each time Arthur's response was the same. Finally, however, the messenger reported that the tide of the weird little battle had changed. The birds, he said, were now defeating the squires. This time it was Arthur who asked Owain to call off his birds, to which the knight replied, with a grin, that it was now the king's move.

Clearly frustrated, Arthur ended the game and turned his attention to his soldiers and the ongoing battle preparations. As the thousands of troops began testing their weapons, the surge of noise flooded Rhonabwy's senses, and he woke up with a start to find himself still lying in Heilyn's dirty, pest-ridden shack. It seemed to Rhonabwy that the events of the extremely peculiar dream had transpired in less than an hour. He was shocked, therefore, when Heilyn told him he had "slept three nights and three days."[47]

Customs Pertaining to Hospitality

Modern literary scholars and historians first encountered *The Dream of Rhonabwy* in 1838. In that year Guest, a noted English authority on the ancient Welsh language, introduced the initial volume of the first published translation of

Geoffrey's Role in the Spread of Arthur's Myths

In 1999 the popular American website about British history and culture, Britannia.com, interviewed Geoffrey Ashe, often hailed as the world's leading Arthurian scholar. The interviewer pointed out that little was known about Arthur and his legends outside the Celtic areas of southern Britain before Geoffrey of Monmouth published the History of the Kings of Britain *in the 1130s. This work inspired subsequent writers, including Chrétien de Troyes and Thomas Malory,* to produce their own versions of Arthur's exploits. Without Geoffrey, the interviewer asked, would people today have even heard of Arthur, and "does Geoffrey, ultimately, deserve all the credit?" Ashe replied:

It's always risky to guess at what would have happened if things had gone otherwise. But Arthur's fame before Geoffrey was strictly among the Welsh, Cornish and Bretons, the Celtic peoples of the west, descended from Britons of his own time or apparent time. If Geoffrey hadn't expanded the saga into a "history" that was read throughout most of Europe, it might have stayed regional and never inspired authors outside. The Irish had a hero something like Arthur, Finn MacCool, and stories of Finn spread to Scotland, but that's as far as they went. No one like Geoffrey took him up, and he never attained international renown as Arthur did.

Quoted in Britannia.com. "A Conversation with Geoffrey Ashe." www.britannia.com/history/h17a.html.

British scholar Geoffrey Ashe (pictured) is considered the world's leading Arthurian scholar.

the *Mabinogion.* As they still do today, the experts eagerly debated the meaning of the obscure and very odd tale about Rhonabwy's encounter with Arthur. As a result, several different possible explanations of the story emerged.

Nevertheless, almost all scholars have come to agree on a couple of points. One deals with the myth's depiction of hospitality, specifically Heilyn's poor treatment of his three guests on the night of the storm. Most medieval Celts who were familiar with the tale likely reacted with disdain on hearing how he broke society's almost ironclad rules surrounding the practice of welcoming of strangers into one's home.

First, unlike the vast majority of Celts, including the poorest ones, Heilyn kept a filthy house, which made his guests uncomfortable. Second, he was openly rude to Rhonabwy and his companions. There was a genuine need among the ancient Celts "to offer food and drink before finding out a visitor's business,"[48] Barry Cunliffe points out. The rigorous rules of Celtic hospitality, he says, were sometimes manipulated by Romans and other foreign peoples. Some enemies of a local Celtic tribe would disguise themselves as innocent travelers and seek shelter in a Celtic home. Then, during the customary welcoming meal, the intruders would produce weapons and slaughter their unsuspecting hosts.

"In all these cases," Cunliffe continues, "the Celtic peoples were bound by custom and tradition to a system involving trust, which their opponents simply abused for their own advantage."[49] In marked contrast to Heilyn in the myth, Arthur displayed the proper hospitality to Rhonabwy. When the latter entered the king's camp, he was immediately offered food and drink and a place to relax. The tale's original author plainly wanted to contrast the proper customs of hospitality in traditional Celtic society with the improper ones.

Awaiting the Call

Rhonabwy's myth also introduced its listeners to some important traditions relating to Arthur and his widely respected knights. First, those listeners did not interpret Rhonabwy's adventure with Arthur simply as part of a dream, as people today typically do. Instead, the Celts believed that after going to sleep, Rhonabwy entered a classic Otherworld in which Arthur resided. In that mystical realm, Rhonabwy witnessed the master of Camelot and his men preparing for one of the largest military engagements of their careers—the battle at Mount Badon. (If a real event, it probably took place sometime between A.D. 490 and 517.) There Arthur was said to have led the natives of the region against a horde of invaders, variously identified as Saxons, Angles, and/or other Germanic peoples from mainland Europe.

However, Rhonabwy never saw Arthur actually leaving for battle. Instead, the sleeping knight awoke as that event was about to happen. During Rhonabwy's stay in the dreamlike Otherworld, Arthur seemed to be only biding his time. His sole interest was to play chess while an absurd and largely harmless battle between squires and birds raged somewhere else in that strange, supernatural sphere.

Based on these facts, the general consensus of modern experts is that Rhonabwy's dream was a vision of a special mythical place. It was none other than the hidden locale where, many legends claimed, Arthur retired after he was badly wounded in his final battle (at Camlann, where he fought his son, Mordred). There Arthur patiently waited, and maybe still waits, for the call to return to the real world and aid righteous causes once more. As researcher Gjoll Hobkynsson puts it, some writers have suggested "that Arthur is a sleeping lord who is waiting to be woken by the sound of supernatural horn. Upon waking from his long sleep Arthur [will] ride with his knights to rid Britain of the Saxon invaders. Some say Arthur resides in the fairy otherworld where he is healing his wounds."[50]

Comparing Peredur to Percival

The Welsh myth *Peredur, Son of Evrawc*, which appears in the *Mabinogion*, is similar in a number of ways to Chrétien de Troyes's romance, *Percival, the Story of the Grail*. One major difference is that the Welsh version does not deal with the Grail.

Tales of Love and Adventure

Another of the tales in the *Mabinogion* that deals with Arthur and his knights is titled *Peredur, Son of Evrawc*. Peredur is the medieval Welsh Celtic name of the English hero Percival—one of Arthur's greatest knights. Percival plays a major role in the more familiar Arthurian myths composed by medieval English and French writers, in particular those involving quests for the Grail (a sacred cup).

The Welsh myth about Peredur does not involve the Grail, however. It deals mainly with that young man's desire to become an Arthurian knight and the adventures he experiences while trying to attain that lofty goal. After Evrawc died when his son was a toddler, Peredur's mother raised him in seclusion, hoping to keep him safe from harm in what she viewed as a much too dangerous world. However, by chance the boy met some of Arthur's knights and became determined to join their order.

Peredur went to Arthur's castle and applied to become a knight. At first, one of the king's leading knights, Sir Kay, ridiculed Peredur because he was poorly dressed. But over time the young man performed numerous impressive deeds, proving himself to both Kay and Arthur. Peredur also met the woman he would later come to love with all his heart, Lady Angharad Golden-Hand.

The relationship between another of Arthur's knights, Geraint, and the woman he loved is the central feature of a third romantic myth from the *Mabinogion*, titled *Geraint and Enid*. In the tale the young Geraint married Enid, and they were happy for a time. But eventually he suspected she was secretly seeing another man. Only through a series of adventures the couple shared did she prove that she was indeed faithful to her husband. In the course of these events, Geraint was badly wounded, and Arthur brought his entire court to Geraint's bedside and waited there for more than a month as the brave knight recovered.

Arthur a Celtic Leader?

As Geraint's and Peredur's tales show, Arthur himself usually does not play a major role in Arthurian myths collected in the *Mabinogion*. Yet his kingdom, royal court, assembly of knights, and gallant reputation are all well established in these Welsh tales, which were written down in mid-to-late medieval times. That fact suggests that the initial Celtic oral traditions on which those writings were based originated several centuries earlier.

In turn this raises the question of whether Arthur's character in those stories is purely fictional or whether that mythical Arthur was based on a real ancient Celtic leader. To begin trying to answer that question, some experts consulted the earliest surviving historical source that mentions Arthur. It is the anonymous *Annales Cambriae*, or *Welsh Annals*, dat-

ing from the late A.D. 700s or early 800s. One entry mentions the date 518 and calls it the year of "the Battle of Badon, in which Arthur bore the cross of our Lord Jesus Christ on his shoulders for three days and three nights, and the Britons were the victors." Here scholars assume that "Badon" is a reference to Mount Badon, the traditional site of Arthur's defeat of an invading enemy army. Another entry in the *Annals*

An illustration depicts Arthur and Mordred in mortal combat at the battle of Camlann in A.D. 539.

pinpoints 539 and claims it was the year of the "Battle of Camlann, in which Arthur and Mordred perished."[51]

If reasonably accurate, these dates may be telling. Rome abandoned its province in England in A.D. 410, leaving its mix of native Celts and Romans on their own. In the decades that followed, various Germanic tribes from continental Europe began threatening the British Isles. The natives badly needed effective military leaders to fend off these threats, and a number of scholars think that Arthur arose to fill this need.

If Arthur *was* a real person, Ashe says, he was not a medieval English king, as so often pictured in novels and movies. Instead, "he really belongs in the late fifth century or the early sixth, a mysterious phase after Britain broke away from the Roman Empire." Ashe adds that some old legendary accounts of Arthur "as a guerrilla fighter, as a military commander, [and] as a benevolent sovereign . . . could all be rooted in memories of successive phases in his career."[52]

The Sarmatian Connection

Numerous theories attempting to identify a historical Arthur from the period in question have been proposed by scholars and nonscholars alike. None has been accepted by a majority of historians. But one that has attracted much attention in recent years suggests that Arthur was a native Celt or Roman (or perhaps both through intermarriage) who carried on an older military tradition. That tradition originated in the late second century A.D., when Marcus Aurelius was emperor of Rome. He defeated the Sarmatians, a tribal people from what is now southern Ukraine. Aurelius was much impressed with the Sarmatian mounted warriors and brought several thousand of them into Rome's military ranks.

A contingent of these foreign cavalrymen were assigned to Roman Britain, where they mingled with the Celts, to whom they were culturally similar. During the three centuries that followed their arrival, they almost certainly blended into the local population. Yet it appears that they proudly kept alive their old cavalry traditions. One way they could have done so was to ensure that at least one person in each new generation of a family became a horseman in local Roman military units. Later, when Rome abandoned Britain, those families remained. They continued turning out young cavalrymen, but now those fighters entered the forces that native leaders mustered to resist the incursions of Germanic marauders.

In this scenario the person who eventually became the model for Arthur was a talented commander of these local mounted warriors. He may have borne the military title or rank of Artorius, a term derived from the name of the first commander of the Sarmatian band assigned to Britain in the second century—Lucius Artorius Castus. It is striking that *Artorius* is the Latin version of the English name Arthur.

Also significant is the fact that in the Arthurian myths, Arthur and his knights carried standards, or banners, featuring images of dragons. According to Arthurian scholar Linda A. Malcor, the leading proponent of the theory connecting Arthur to the Sarmatians, "Roman military units had their own standards," including "auxiliary units like the Sarmatians." She points out that "the standard used by the Sarmatians happened to be a bronze dragonhead."[53]

Sarmatian cavalry are shown here on Trajan's column in Rome. The Roman emperor Marcus Aurelius conquered them and sent a Sarmatian contingent to serve in Roman-controlled Britain, where they intermingled with the Celts.

Malcor and other experts who advocate the Sarmatian connection to the historical Celtic Arthur propose that the mythical king was a combination of two different men. Some of the feats attributed to Arthur in the myths, they say, may have been cultural memories of deeds performed by the heroic cavalry officer Lucius Artorius Castus in the second century. Other Arthurian exploits in the myths were those of a fifth-century cavalry leader of the Celtic-Roman descendants of the first Sarmatians who settled in Britain. Over time, Malcor suggests, the merger of stories about the two men and their accomplishments became seamless in the ongoing and expanding stream of Arthurian legends.

To Believe or Disbelieve?

The theory "cannot account for every detail in the Arthurian legends," Malcor admits. Still, she says, "the parallels between Castus and Arthur are striking not only in their number but also in the variety of levels on which they occur." The mythical Arthur "meets all of the qualifications required for him to be the historical catalyst for the legends," she writes, plus he lived in the right historical period. These factors make "Castus a powerful candidate for the title of the historical Arthur."[54]

Even if Malcor's identification of the mythical Arthur is incorrect, several other plausible candidates for a real Celtic version of him have been proposed. In fact, Ashe stated in a 1999 interview, historians regularly look for and frequently find connections between legends and real life. They are not surprised by such finds because throughout history people have spun yarns that exaggerated and embellished the characters and deeds of popular or interesting people. "The Arthurian [literary and cultural] phenomenon is a fact, a very big and complex fact," Ashe said. "Until someone proves conclusively that Arthur was not a real person, I'd say it remains easier on balance to believe in him than to disbelieve."[55]

CHAPTER 5

The Celtic Myths in Popular Culture

The long-lived, mysterious world of the ancient Celts was not fated to survive. Over the relentless march of centuries, ancient times morphed into the medieval interlude, which itself eventually gave way to the modern era. First the old Celtic ways waned. In some places they died out, while in others they blended into newer, more dominant cultures.

Through all this unremitting change, a number of the ancient Celtic customs, beliefs, and vibrant myths persisted in Europe. But many of them were forgotten or lost, never to be rediscovered by curious later ages. In some cases, moreover, these losses of cultural ideas were the result of purposeful sabotage. Legions of Christian priests viewed some of the old beliefs and stories as pagan. To their narrow minds, that made them potentially corruptive influences on society, so they trashed some of the tales altogether and altered others to render them acceptable.

Survival via Oral Means

Nevertheless, the final death knell had not yet sounded for Celtic mythology. Via oral means, a certain number of the original Celtic myths did survive the ravages of time and

Celtic stories and traditions were passed down orally from generation to generation by bards, or storytellers, such as the one shown here entertaining the people.

human mischief. In century after century in Ireland, for instance, traditional storytellers continued to transmit the old myths to members of each new generation. As early as the 50s B.C., Julius Caesar had observed such oral transmission of culture in action. Speaking of the Druids he encountered in Gaul, Caesar wrote, "They are said to learn a great number of verses by heart—so many, in fact, that some people spend twenty years"[56] listening to them recite the verses.

Nearly two thousand years later, a noted expert on Western folklore, J.H. Delargy, closely studied this phenomenon.

He recalled that as late as the 1920s a seventy-year-old fisherman named Sean O'Conaill was still fulfilling this role of community storyteller in County Kerry, in southwestern Ireland. With a sense of wonder and admiration, Delargy pointed out that O'Conaill was illiterate, yet

> he was one of the best-read men in the unwritten literature of the people whom I have ever known. His mind [was] a storehouse of traditions of all kinds, pithy anecdotes [brief stories], and intricate hero-tales, proverbs and rhymes and riddles, and other features of the rich orally preserved lore common to all Ireland three hundred years ago. He was a conscious literary artist. He took a deep pleasure in telling his tales. His language was clear and vigorous, and had in it the stuff of literature.[57]

Through the continued practice of this venerable ancient art of storytelling, a fair number of the ancient tales of Celtic gods and heroes seemingly refused to die. In an almost unrelenting torrent, they flowed forward through the centuries. Some of them came together in early modern myth collections, like the *Mabinogion*, which Lady Charlotte Guest so earnestly and carefully pieced together.

Others worked their way into every form of literature, art, and communication conceived by each succeeding age. As a result, modern popular culture in the Western world abounds with these myths. They loom in images on movie and television screens and in comic books and video games as well as on the printed page. The Tuatha, Cuchulain, Finn McCool, Arthur, and others live on, ageless, endlessly appealing, and still able to capture the human imagination.

Reborn in Sculptures and Paintings

Thanks to the survival of these colorful myths in the modern era, several of the old Celtic deities and heroes were, in a sense, reborn to fascinate and entertain new generations of devoted admirers. Often the gods and human warriors

A Celt Captured in Stone

Of the many artistic renditions of the ancient Celts and their heroes created over the centuries, none is more famous than *The Dying Gaul*. This magnificent stone sculpture is thought to be a Roman copy of a Greek bronze statue made in the 200s B.C. It shows a mortally wounded Celtic warrior resting on his side.

of the long-dead ancient Celts have been depicted in the arts of sculpture and painting. The life-size stone statue called *The Dying Gaul*, a moving rendition of a wounded Celtic warrior, is one of the more famous examples. It was first carved by an ancient Roman sculptor and fell into obscurity when the Roman Empire disintegrated. But the work was rediscovered in modern times, and today copies of it can be found in museums, universities, courthouses, and other public buildings across the Western world.

In 1911 a modern Irish sculptor, Oliver Sheppard, gave the world another timeless statue of a dying Celtic fighter—this one the most imposing warrior in all of the surviving Celtic myths. Titled *The Death of Cuchulain* (sometimes also called *The Dying Cuchulain*), it rests in the General Post Office in Dublin, Ireland. The huge bronze work shows the mighty hero perishing in the midst of battle. His muscular body is still attached to the large rock to which he had tied himself so he could maintain his honor by dying on his feet.

The daring and ever-popular Cuchulain has also been the subject of seemingly countless modern paintings and illustrations. One of the most familiar and beautiful is an illustration showing him, his spear raised above his head, riding his formidable chariot into battle. Created by American artist J.C. Leyendecker, it first appeared in Irish writer T.W. Rolleston's 1911 book *Myths and Legends of the Celtic Race*. But the image has been reproduced countless times in books and magazines ever since.

Celtic Arthurian heroes have also been frequently captured on modern artists' canvases. Subsequently, those images have been reproduced in books; websites; the covers of magazines, record albums, and CDs; and other venues of popular culture. Particularly popular in this artistic genre are the Arthurian-inspired paintings of the great nineteenth-century English artist George Frederic Watts. Although he captured numerous modern subjects in his work, he is best known for his lushly rendered images of characters from Greek, Roman, and Celtic mythology. Of the latter, his 1862 painting of Sir Galahad standing beside a splendid white horse is one of the most renowned.

A more recent surge of artistic depictions of Celtic mythical lore began in the 1960s and 1970s. In those decades interest in alternative religions and the occult became widespread in Western culture. Hundreds and eventually thousands of artists began turning out paintings of gods, fairies, monsters, mythical heroes, and other denizens of the ancient Celtic Otherworlds.

One of the best-known and most widely popular of these artists is American illustrator and painter Howard David Johnson, born in 1954. Known for his mythological subjects, he often employs mixed media in his works. This includes ingenious and striking combinations of photographic and painted images. Among the ancient Celtic gods Johnson has

This stone statue of a mortally wounded Celtic warrior was carved by a Roman sculptor and is titled The Dying Gaul.

J.C. Leyendecker's illustration of Culchulain shows the Celtic hero riding his chariot into battle.

masterfully captured are the mother goddess Danu, who gave rise to the Tuatha; that group's father figure, the Dagda; and the deities Lugh and Brigid. The artist has also produced canvases showing the legendary heroes Cuchulain and Finn McCool. Johnson's Celtic paintings are regularly displayed on the covers of books and CDs, in movies and television shows, and in the background images in computer games and software.

Yeats, Poetry, and Nationalism

Literature went hand in hand with painting and other arts as a venue for modern revivals and explorations of the characters and events of ancient Celtic myths. The first major surge of Celtic-themed literature occurred in the poetry genre. Among the dozens of talented English, Irish, French, and American poets who produced such works, one of the most widely known and respected was Irishman William Butler Yeats. Today he is universally recognized as one of the leading literary figures of the late nineteenth and early twentieth centuries.

As a boy Yeats developed a strong fascination for the old Celtic gods and heroes, and as a young man he began expressing that interest in poems. In 1889 he published his first series of poetic works about Celtic themes in *The Wanderings of Oisin and Other Poems*. The work mentioned in the title deals with Finn McCool's son, Oisin, who was known as an excellent poet in his own right. For a taste of Yeats's flowing, luxuriant verses—which seem to fall easily off the tongue when read aloud—one need not search further than this ode to the Fenian hunters in his poem about Oisin:

> In what far kingdom do you go'
> Ah Fenians, with the shield and bow?
> Or are you phantoms white as snow,
> Whose lips had life's most prosperous glow?
> O you, with whom in sloping valleys,
> Or down the dewy forest alleys,
> I chased at morn the flying deer,
> With whom I hurled the hurrying spear,
> And heard the foemen's bucklers rattle,
> And broke the heaving ranks of battle![58]

Over time, as Yeats continued to turn out writings about the ancient Celtic gods and heroes, they increasingly took on an air of Irish nationalism. Indeed, they strongly resonated with those Irish who lobbied and fought for independence

The Irish poet William Butler Yeats published his first poems with Celtic themes in 1889 in his Wanderings of Oisin, and Other Poems.

from Britain in the early years of the twentieth century. One modern researcher of Yeats's work explains:

> By incorporating into his work the stories and characters of Celtic origin, Yeats endeavored to encapsulate [summarize] something of the national character of his beloved Ireland. The reasons and motivations for Yeats' use of Celtic themes can be understood in terms of the author's own sense of nationalism as well as an overriding personal interest in mythology and the oral traditions of folklore. . . . The folklore, myth, and legends of ancient Celtic traditions gave Yeats a rich well of inspiration to draw from. By not falling into the trap of overly romanticizing his work, as many other authors of the time would do, Yeats was able to help begin a tradition of another sort, the Irish literary tradition. By placing importance on the Irish culture in his work, Yeats fulfilled his own sense of national pride to the delight of his readers and audiences.[59]

Maintaining Beliefs from an Ancient Past

One of the more important ancient Celtic cultural customs related to mythical beliefs was periodically remembering the memory of deceased loved ones and community members. Despite the passage of many centuries, it remains very much alive in Brittany, a cultural region of northwestern France that was once a major Celtic enclave. Perhaps more than anywhere else, Brittany displays a sense of cultural continuity with its pre-Christian Celtic past. The custom in question centers on Toussaint, or All Saints, celebrated each year on November 1. Preparations begin days or sometimes weeks before, when volunteers thoroughly clean churchyards and cemeteries and fill them with flowers. Toussaint occurs directly after the All Saints (also called Hallows) Eve, on October 31 which was merged with the Celtic harvest celebration of Samhain and has become Halloween. During Samhain, it was thought that the legendary spirits of the dead could and often did return briefly to visit, and in some cases haunt, the living. These and some other ancient Celtic social customs have survived to one degree or another in various parts of Europe and the British Isles. Beside the All Saints Church in North Yorkshire, England, for example, stands a tall stone monolith thought to be thousands of years old. People still visit the pillar hoping to take advantage of an ancient mystical tradition, says Richard Jones, author of *Haunted Britain and Ireland*. It holds "that if a man touches the stone with his wedding ring on three successive nights when the moon is waxing, he will become a more effective lover."

Richard Jones. *Myths and Legends of Britain and Ireland.* London: New Holland, 2003, p. 136.

Revelers are silhouetted against the fires of Bonfire Night, celebrating the beginning of the Celtic festival of Samhain.

Diving into Uncharted Territory

Another literary area that has abounded with modern adaptations and interpretations of the old Celtic myths is the fantasy novel market. Novelists who specialize in fantasy have generated many hundreds of works in that specialized and widely popular field. Of these an outstanding example is the *Age of Misrule*, a trilogy of books by English novelist and screenwriter Mark Chadbourn. A noted author of science fiction and fantasy, he has won the coveted British Fantasy Award twice (in 2005 and 2007).

The three volumes in the *Age of Misrule* series are *World's End* (1999), *Darkest Hour* (2000), and *Always Forever* (2001). The story they tell is set in modern Britain, where two strangers, a man and woman, are suddenly drawn together by a horrific shared experience. They find themselves pulled into a series of apocalyptic (world-threatening) events. Giants, dragons, and other supposedly mythical creatures have materialized very much in the flesh in various places and begun to kill people. At the same time, most modern technology no longer works. Moreover, and no less surprisingly, magical spells like those described in ancient myths *do* seem to work.

Frantically searching for an explanation, the leading characters discover a frightening fact. The Fomorians, the hideous beasts who were said to have ruled Ireland in primeval times, are about to return to earth, where they will destroy or enslave humanity. Furthermore, the Tuatha De Danann, the ancient race of Irish gods, are also on the verge of revisiting the world. Although these deities are the Fomorians' mortal enemies, they are not necessarily humans' natural allies, which does not bode well for the fate of the modern world.

Chadbourn develops this simultaneously stimulating and disturbing premise with both skill and imagination. Noted English book reviewer Nathan Brazil aptly said of the entire trilogy that

> This is not a story which involves noble elves doing good deeds, cute little blokes with furry feet, or scruffy sods claiming to be the returned king. The ingenious premise questions what might happen to our reality if the gods of Celtic mythology returned, slap bang into

the middle of the modern world. Does it signal the end of the age of science? These questions dive head first off the standard fantasy diving board, into relatively uncharted territory, resulting in an edge of the seat, highly credible, page turner which I found compulsive reading.[60]

Cuchulain's Many Modern Faces

Another of Celtic mythology's major characters has returned to the world in a different manner than the one Chadbourn depicts. The Irish super-warrior Cuchulain reemerged in the modern era in numerous venues of modern popular culture. As a result, he came to play several roles he did not play in ancient myths, thereby requiring him to wear what amounts to many new faces.

Finn Entertains Children in Maine

During the nineteenth, twentieth, and early twenty-first centuries, a number of plays were written or adapted that depict characters and stories from the ancient Celtic myths. Among the more recent examples was the production of a stage show titled *The Legend of Finn MacCool*. It appeared in May 2013 at the Theater at Monmouth, a project of the Rangeley Friends of the Arts (RFA), in Rangeley, Maine. The production was aimed at young people as both an entertainment piece and educational experience. RFA's official website explains that the play

> was adapted to build analytical and literacy skills through the exploration of verse and playwriting,

fostering creativity and inspiring imaginative thinking. *The Legend of Finn MacCool* is composed of three tales about the legendary third-century hero from Ireland. These tales were selected to explore what helped make Finn a good friend, good neighbor, and good citizen. After the performance, students were engaged in a question and answer session with the actors.

The RFA production about Finn shows how some of the old Celtic myths can still be both relevant and entertaining to modern audiences.

Rangeley Friends of the Arts. "*Finn MacCool* Performed by Theater at Monmouth." http://rangeleyarts.org/finn-mccool-performed-by-theater-at-monmouth.

To modern Irish patriots, Cuchulain serves as the model of an individual who stands up to outside forces bent on destroying his country.

One modern arena into which Cuchulain's modern admirers have thrust him is that of national politics. In the same way that some of Yeats's poems did, memories of the ancient hero's feats fueled feelings of nationalism among Irish rebels who sought independence from Great Britain in the early 1900s. To those modern Irish patriots, Cuchulain was a model of an individual who stood up to outside forces that threatened to destroy his country and the way of life of its citizens. "His stoical acts of physical resistance, even when outnumbered," historian Nuala C.

Johnson writes, "resonated with the public's perception of the"[61] Irish uprising.

In the years that followed this political unrest, painters, sculptors, musical composers, and other kinds of artists regularly depicted Cuchulain and his deeds. Among the many musical pieces generated in that period was Scottish composer Ronald Center's symphony, titled *The Coming of Cuchulain*. It was first performed in 1944, shortly before the close of World War II. In 1994 the same ancient character inspired a song in the widely popular theatrical show *Riverdance*, known for its energetic, exciting displays of Irish step dancing. Titled "The Lament of Cuchulain," it is usually played on authentic traditional Irish instruments, including the bagpipe-like uilleann pipes.

Later still, several individual rock songs about the heroic Cuchulain emerged in the British Isles. Prominent among them is "Cattle Raid of Cooley," based on the character's most famous military exploit. The song appears on the album *The Middle Kingdom*, released in 2000 by the trendy Irish heavy metal group Cruachan. (Five years before, the band had released *Tuatha Na Gael*, an album with songs about various Irish gods and myths.)

The Marvelous Marvel Universe

Another modern face of Cuchulain was revealed in the 1990s when Marvel Comics began to feature him as one of the muscular superheroes in its colorful and popular graphic novel universe. Part of the group known as the Guardians of the Galaxy, his character is also sometimes identified by the nickname Irish Wolfhound. Another well-known ancient Irish hero, Finn McCool, also periodically appears in the marvelous Marvel universe. Curiously, however, he portrays an archenemy of Cuchulain, making Finn's character a villain rather than the customary hero he usually plays.

Fortunately for Finn, the sterling reputation as a "good guy" that he enjoyed in the ancient Celtic myths remains intact in several other, largely more serious modern literary genres. Among them is the children's novel, exemplified by two popular books by American writer Mary Tannen. One,

The Wizard Children of Finn (1982), features two contemporary children, a sister and brother. After being transported back to ancient Ireland, they meet the legendary Finn and in the course of the story help him to acquire his reputation as a hero.

Tannen's sequel to her first book about Finn is titled *The Lost Legend of Finn* (1983). In it the same two young people again travel back into the past. This time they find themselves in Ireland in the year 800, where, among other things, they must contend with marauding Vikings. In an especially entertaining twist, they shape-shift into ravens, which allows them to soar through the air. This is one of Tannen's many modern references to the magical abilities possessed by a number of the characters in the old Celtic myths.

Nobody Else like Him

Some of the Celtic gods, along with Cuchulain, Finn, and a few other ancient Celtic heroes, have therefore attained a modest degree of notoriety in modern Western society. Yet only one legendary figure from the entire mythology produced by the ancient Celts is today instantly recognizable to people of all walks of life. That figure is King Arthur, who has long been rumored to still be sleeping in a well-hidden mystical realm, awaiting the call to return to earth and aid the downtrodden.

In fact, only a tiny handful of characters from all of humanity's combined mythologies can match the almost universal familiarity, respect, and admiration that Arthur has acquired over the centuries. Geoffrey Ashe offers an explanation for the character's tremendous continuing popularity, saying that the master of Camelot

> is a distinctive contribution to world mythology. There is nobody else quite like him; no human hero at least. Other legendary sleepers, who may or may not wake up, are very probably imitations of him. And in any case, they do not carry his golden-age quality. What Arthur stands for is the idea of a long-lost glory

or promise, plus a belief that it is not truly lost; that it can be reinstated for a fresh start, with intervening corruption swept away. Belief of that kind is a real and potent motive force which is seldom given due weight as a factor in history.[62]

That almost magical hope or belief that there once existed a truly good and just ruler and that he may someday return to cure society's ills has indeed been powerful over the centuries. After Arthur first appeared as a secondary character in *The Dream of Rhonabwy* and a few other early Welsh myths, his popularity grew. Medieval English and French writers built on those ancient Celtic stories, in the process spinning romantic tales like Malory's *The Death of Arthur*. These works added many new details to the earlier stories about Arthur. They also immortalized that beloved monarch and his virtuous knights in the eyes of new generations of Europeans, in turn inspiring the creation of still more Arthurian writings and myths.

Expanding the Arthurian Mythos

That stream of Arthurian works became a virtual flood in the Victorian era of the nineteenth century (named for Britain's Queen Victoria, who reigned from 1837 to 1901). An outstanding and still widely admired example was Englishman Alfred, Lord Tennyson's series of long poems *Idylls of the King* (1874). Tennyson retold a large number of the then existing Arthurian myths. He also put his own thematic and moralistic spin on the growing Arthurian mythos. Through the lens of Tennyson's writings, Arthur's court became more romantic, sentimental, and ethically idealistic than ever. True, Camelot's ruler, his wife Guinevere, and the knights of the Round Table had featured a moral dimension well before Tennyson. But he expanded it even further, emphasizing Arthur as a force for good who was betrayed by the queen's infidelity with one of his own knights.

Tennyson's *Idylls* was extremely influential among writers and artists of the Victorian age and the decades that followed it. Painters "produced striking paintings based on Arthurian themes," literary scholar John Matthews points out. Also, the noted early photographer Julia Margaret Cameron created "a series of portraits of scenes from Tennyson's poems in which well-known people posed as Arthurian characters," says Matthews. "Poetry, good, bad, and indifferent, imitating Tennyson, poured forth and was avidly read. Plays and pageants were performed all over [Britain and France] depicting the adventures of Arthur and his knights."[63]

As the cultural influences of and references to Arthur and his mythical kingdom persisted in the twentieth century, they increasingly kindled the interest of people of all ages and backgrounds in Western society. Arthurian lore became a fashionable mystique that writers, artists, and entertainers felt comfortable exploiting. In addition, Arthur's legendary goodness and chivalry plucked at people's heartstrings, making him increasingly romantic and beloved as time went on.

This larger-than-life, upbeat image made Arthur the perfect hero for modern novels, as well as for a hugely expressive new art form—the motion picture. In fact, the new novels about Arthur often *became* movies. For example, renowned American humorist Mark Twain's clever novel *A Connecticut Yankee in King Arthur's Court* was made into a silent film in 1921, a sound version in 1931, and a movie musical in 1949. Numerous other films about Arthur and his knights were made as well, among them *Knights of the Round Table* (1953) and *Prince Valiant* (1954, based on a comic strip about Arthur's court).

The Power of Myth

To many people in the mid-1950s it seemed that the cultural celebration of Arthur and his world had reached its peak. However, it soon became clear that the modern fascination for his myths had only just begun to emerge. The year 1958 witnessed the appearance of the twentieth century's Arthurian equivalent of the nineteenth century's *Idylls of the King*.

The pivotal work in question was English writer T.H. White's novel *The Once and Future King*. White told the age-old story of Arthur in great detail and from the very beginning. The novel's narrative follows Arthur's adventures as a young boy learning about the enchanted world of his birth from his mysterious mentor, Merlin; Arthur's early manhood; and his conception of the Round Table and gathering of his trusty knights. It also depicts his stormy relationships with

Author T.H. White's novel The Once and Future King *stands as one of the best works on the Arthurian legends.*

the queen; her lover, Sir Lancelot; and Arthur's son, Mordred, who ends up betraying him. All of these figures became more complex in White's hands, as well as more modern. The novel made them characters that people living in the twentieth century could identify with and come to love.

Not surprisingly, White's reimagined Arthurian universe was extremely influential and immediately began generating spinoffs. The first was the great 1960 Broadway musical *Camelot*, which featured Richard Burton as Arthur and a young Julie Andrews as Guinevere. That play became a major feature film in 1967. It starred Richard Harris as Arthur and Vanessa Redgrave as his queen. Meanwhile, in 1965 Walt Disney released a feature-length cartoon *The Sword in the Stone*, based directly on the opening sections of White's novel.

More Arthurian films followed, and today new books, movies, and TV versions of the characters and tales from the Arthurian mythos continue to appear on a regular basis. These and the other modern adaptations of legendary Celtic figures and stories clearly demonstrate the power of myth on both the human mind and human society. Ideas born long ago in tales told by word of mouth around hearths in homes made of thatch slowly but steadily made their way down the corridors of time and an ever-changing world. The ancient Celts themselves are long since gone. Yet the tales of gods and heroes that comforted them and fired their imaginations live on among their distant descendants and countless other people who love to hear a good story and pass it on to others.

NOTES

Introduction: Three Basic Celtic Questions

1. Kathryn Hinds and Francine Nicholson. "The Story Behind the Stories: Celtic Mythology and Folklore." Land, Sea and Sky. http://homepage.eircom.net/~shae/chapter7.htm.

2. Juliette Wood. *The Celts: Life, Myth, and Art*. New York: Stewart, Tabori, and Chang, 1998, p. 10.

3. Julius Caesar. *Commentaries on the Gallic War*. In *War Commentaries of Caesar*, translated by Rex Warner. New York: New American Library, 1960, p. 124.

4. Laura Foreman et al. *Celts: Europe's People of Iron*. Alexandria, VA: Time-Life, 1994, pp. 130–131.

5. Hinds and Nicholson. "The Story Behind the Stories."

6. Hinds and Nicholson. "The Story Behind the Stories."

Chapter 1: Customs and Lives of the Ancient Celts

7. Jen Green. *Ancient Celts: Archaeology Unlocks the Secrets of the Celts'* Past. Washington, DC: National Geographic Society, 2008, pp. 41–42.

8. Foreman. *Celts*, p. 45.

9. Barry Cunliffe. "In Search of the Celts." In *The Celts*, by Nora Chadwick. London: Penguin, 1971, p. 20.

10. Pliny the Elder. *Natural History*. Vol. 3. Translated by John Bostock and H.T. Riley. London: George Bell and Sons, 1890, p. 103.

11. Barry Cunliffe. *The Ancient Celts*. New York: Oxford University Press, 2000, p. 74.

12. Ammianus Marcellinus. *History*. Published as *The Later Roman Empire, A.D. 354–378*. Translated and edited by Walter Hamilton. New York: Penguin, 2001, p. 85.

13. Quoted in M.I. Ebbutt. *Hero-Myths and Legends of the British Race*. Calgary, AB: Theophania, 2011, pp. 191–192.

14. Barry Cunliffe. *The Celts: A Very Sort Introduction*. New York: Oxford University Press, 2003, p. 56.

15. Caesar. *Commentaries on the Gallic War*, p. 123.

16. Wood. *The Celts*, p. 126.

17. Cunliffe. *The Ancient Celts*, p. 89.

18. David Leeming. *From Olympus to Camelot: The World of European Mythology*. New York: Oxford University Press, 2005, p. 30.

19. Arthur E.R. Boak. *A History of Rome to 565 A.D.* Hong Kong: Forgotten Books, 2013, p. 51.

20. Plutarch. *Life of Camillus*. In *Plutarch's Lives*, translated by John Dryden. New York: Random House, 2001, p. 165.

Chapter 2: Tales of the Celtic Cosmos and Gods

21. Quoted in Augusta Gregory. *Gods and Fighting Men: The Story of the Tuatha De Danaan and of the Fianna of Ireland*. Cedar Lake, MI: Read a Classic, 2010, p. 22.

22. Miranda J. Green. *Celtic Myths*. Austin: University of Texas Press, 2001, p. 18.

23. Kuno Meyer, ed. and trans. *The Voyage of Bran*. London: David Nutt, 1895, pp. 6, 8.

24. Quoted in Gregory. *Gods and Fighting Men*, p. 126.

25. Gregory. *Gods and Fighting Men*, p. 129.

26. Green. *Celtic Myths*, p. 37.

27. Peter B. Ellis. *Celtic Myths and Legends*. New York: Carroll and Graf, 2004, p. 21.

28. Arthur Cotterell. *Celtic Mythology: The Myths and Legends of the Celtic World*. London: Lorenz, 2000, p. 23.

29. Ellis. *Celtic Myths and Legends*, p. 20.

Chapter 3: Memorable Mythical Celtic Heroes

30. Christopher R. Fee. *Gods, Heroes, and Kings: The Battle for Mythic Britain*. New York: Oxford University Press, 2004, p. 191.

31. Quoted in Richard Barber. *Myths and Legends of the British Isles*. New York: Barnes and Noble, 2004, p. 90.

32. Barber. *Myths and Legends*, p. 100.

33. Quoted in Barber. *Myths and Legends*, p. 100.

34. David James. *Celtic Connections: The Ancient Celts, Their Tradition and Living Legacy*. London: Cassell, 1996, p. 44.

35. Homer. *Iliad*. Translated by W.H.D. Rouse. New York: Signet, 2007, p. 110.

36. Quoted in Cotterell. *Celtic Mythology*, p. 34.

37. Augusta Gregory. *Cuchulain of Muirthemne: The Story of the Men of the Red Branch of Ulster*. Charleston, SC: Forgotten Books, 2007, p. 10.

38. Anonymous. *The Cattle Raid of Cooley*. Published as *The Tain*. Translated by Thomas Kinsella. Oxford: Oxford University Press, 2002, pp. 150–152.

39. Proinsias Mac Cana. *Celtic Mythology*. New York: Bedrick, 1987, p. 107.

40. Charles Squire. *Celtic Myth and Legend*. Franklin Lakes, NJ: New Page, 2001, pp. 203–204.

41. Squire. *Celtic Myth and Legend*, p. 206.

Chapter 4: Early Arthurian Characters and Tales

42. Geoffrey Ashe. *Mythology of the British Isles*. New York: Methuen, 2002, pp. 98–99.

43. Barber. *Myths and Legends*, p. xi.

44. Charlotte E. Guest, trans. *The Mabinogion and Other Ancient Welsh Manuscripts*. London: Longmans, 1838–1849, p. 394.

45. Guest. *The Mabinogion*, pp. 394–395.

46. Guest. *The Mabinogion*, p. 398.

47. Guest. *The Mabinogion*, p. 409.

48. Cunliffe. *The Ancient Celts*, p. 107.

49. Cunliffe. *The Ancient Celts*, p. 107.

50. Gjoll Hobkynsson. "The Celts and Saxons: A Barbarian Conspiracy." Druid Grove, the Order of Bards, Ovates & Druids. www.druidry.org /library/miscellaneous/celts-and -saxons-barbarian-conspiracy.

51. Quoted in Richard Barber, ed. *The Arthurian Legends: An Illustrated Anthology*. Rochester, NY: Boydell, 1996, p. 7.

52. Quoted in Britannia.com. "A Conversation with Geoffrey Ashe." www.britannia.com/history/h17a .html.

53. Linda A. Malcor. "Lucius Artorius Castus: Part 2: The Battles in Britain." *Heroic Age*, Autumn/Winter 1999. www.mun.ca/mst/heroicage /issues/2/ha2lac.htm.

54. Malcor. "Lucius Artorius Castus."

55. Quoted in Britannia.com. "A Conversation with Geoffrey Ashe."

Chapter 5: The Celtic Myths in Popular Culture

56. Caesar. *Commentaries on the Gallic War*, p. 123.

57. J.H. Delargy. "The Gaelic Storyteller." *Ireland of the Welcomes*, January 1952, p. 3.

58. William Butler Yeats. "The Wanderings of Oisin, Book 1." California State University–Northridge. www.csun.edu/~hceng029/yeats /yeatspoems/WanderingsOfOi.

59. Matthew Bell. "Yeats, Nationalism, and Myth." Writing@CSU. http:// writing.colostate.edu.

60. Nathan Brazil. "Review of *The Age of Misrule*." SF Site. http://www.sf site.com/01a/am191.htm.

61. Nuala C. Johnson. *Ireland, the Great War, and the Geography of*

Remembrance. New York: Cambridge University Press, 2003, p. 151.

62. Ashe. *Mythology of the British Isles*, p. 306.

63. John Matthews. *King Arthur: Dark Age Warrior and Mythic Hero*. New York: Random House, 2004, pp. 108–109.

caricature: A rough sketch or cartoon version of a character.

cauldron: A large metal pot used for cooking or boiling water. The ancient Celts believed that cauldrons sometimes had magical properties.

cosmos: The universe.

currach: A small boat made of ox hide stretched across a wooden frame. Currachs were common in the British Isles in medieval times.

Druid: An ancient Celtic priest.

fiana **(or Fenians):** The band of warriors headed by the ancient Irish hero Finn McCool.

frame story: A literary form in which the plot begins in a certain place and time, later switches—via a character's recollection or dream—to a different setting, and still later returns to the original setting.

Gaul: The Latin (Roman) name for the region now comprising France and Belgium.

Grail: In Arthurian mythology, the cup used by Jesus at the Last Supper. It was thought to have magical properties, so several of Arthur's knights attempted to find it.

gwas: An ancient Celtic word meaning vassal or retainer.

hall: An ancient Celtic word for salt.

hero's portion: In ancient Celtic communal feasts, the parts of the animal being served that were set aside for the strongest warrior present.

immram: An old Irish literary genre that describes adventurous voyages to faraway, unknown islands.

mythos: A large collection of myths and related beliefs and customs surrounding a legendary person, place, or people.

nationalism: Fervid feelings of loyalty and patriotism in a country.

oppida: The ancient Roman term for large Celtic hill forts.

Otherworld: One of many separate, mystical universes recognized in Celtic mythology. Most Otherworlds were invisible to human eyes.

retainer (or vassal): A well-trained warrior who is supported by and personally loyal to a military leader.

sacrifice: An offering or gift made to a god or gods.

smith: An artisan who works with metals.

symphony: A large-scale musical work, usually having four separate movements and scored for a full orchestra.

thatch: Bundled tree branches, straw, or grass often used in building ancient and medieval houses.

torque: A metal necklace that was popular among the ancient Celts.

warp spasm (or killing frenzy): The bizarre, frightening transformation into a monstrous killing machine undergone by the ancient Irish hero Cuchulain as he went into battle.

wattle and daub: A web of wooden strips held together by a glue-like mixture of clay, straw, and/or animal dung, used in building the houses of common folk in the ancient and medieval eras.

Books

Anonymous. *The Cattle Raid of Cooley*. Published as *The Tain*. Translated by Thomas Kinsella. Oxford: Oxford University Press, 2002. This modern translation of one of the most important and complex Celtic myths is both comprehensive and elegantly worded.

Richard Barber. *Myths and Legends of the British Isles*. New York: Barnes and Noble, 2004. A comprehensive collection of ancient British myths, including those of the Saxons, Welsh, Irish, and other early British peoples.

Nora K. Chadwick and Barry Cunliffe. *The Celts*. London: Folio Society, 2008. The authors have compiled one of the best available overviews of Celtic culture, told in easy-to-read prose.

Arthur Cotterell. *Celtic Mythology: The Myths and Legends of the Celtic World*. London: Lorenz, 2000. This first-rate introductory mythology book features an encyclopedia-style alphabetical listing of mythical characters, supported by many beautiful color illustrations.

Arthur Cotterell. *The Illustrated A–Z of Classical Mythology: The Legends of Ancient Greece, Rome, and the Norse and Celtic Worlds*. London: Lorenz, 2013. A larger, more detailed version of Cotterell's earlier book on Celtic mythology.

Barry Cunliffe. *The Celts: A Very Short Introduction*. New York: Oxford University Press, 2003. As the title says, this is a fairly short book, but it is packed with useful information about the Celts.

Peter B. Ellis. *Celtic Myths and Legends*. New York: Carroll and Graf, 2004. This is one of the most comprehensive collections of old Celtic myths available today.

Peter B. Ellis. *Eyewitness to Irish History*. New York: Wiley, 2007. An overview of Irish civilization that contains frequent references to the area's ancient Celtic legends.

Christopher R. Fee. *Gods, Heroes, and Kings: The Battle for Mythic Britain*. New York: Oxford University Press, 2004. The author presents a well-written, detailed exposition of the divine pantheons, heroes, and sacred objects of the Celts, Scandinavians, and other peoples who contributed tales to the mythology of ancient Britain.

Patrick K. Ford, ed. and trans. *The Mabinogi and Other Medieval Welsh Tales. Berkeley*: University of California Press, 2008. This is a highly regarded translation of some of the old Welsh tales, including those of the ancient Celts.

Miranda J. Green. *Celtic Myths*. Austin: University of Texas Press, 2001. A straightforward, easy-to-read compilation of the major Celtic myths and legendary characters.

Miranda J. Green. *The Gods of the Celts*. Gloucestershire, England: History, 2004. This volume focuses on the Celtic deities in more detail than in Green's 2001 study of the Celtic myths.

Richard Jones. *Myths and Legends of Britain and Ireland*. London: New Holland, 2003. A beautifully illustrated, easy-to-read volume that explores the various settings of the old myths of Britain and Ireland.

Daniel Mersy. *King Arthur*. Oxford, England: Osprey, 2013. Retells many of the Arthurian stories in a reader-friendly manner and explores whether Arthur may have been a real person.

Christopher Snyder. *The World of King Arthur*. London: Thames and Hudson, 2011. A well-written and exquisitely illustrated overview of Arthurian history, lore, literature, and more.

Websites

Celtic Gods and Goddesses (www.bel laterreno.com/graphics/clipart_mysti cal/celticgods/default.htm). A colorful collection of images created over the centuries that depict the various deities and heroes of Celtic mythology.

A Conversation with Geoffrey Ashe, Britannia.com (www.britannia.com /history/h17a.html). This site presents an excellent, informational interview with one of the leading scholars of Celtic mythology.

Cuchulain, Marvel Comics (www .marvunapp.com/Appendix/cuchulai. htm). This entertaining site gives all the details for the character that the ancient Celtic hero Cuchulain plays in Marvel Comics' team of superheroes, the Guardians of the Galaxy.

The Dream of Rhonabwy, **Britannia .com** (www.britannia.com/history /docs/rhonabwy.html). A translation of part of the famous early Welsh tale that portrays an early Arthur, before the addition of many of the elements of his myths familiar today.

King Arthur, "Once and Future King," Michael Wood and the BBC (www .bbc.co.uk/history/ancient/anglo _saxons/arthur_01.shtml). A noted author and filmmaker joins forces with the BBC to discuss the major elements of the surviving Arthurian myths.

INDEX

Celts, **18**

    connections between myths and lives of, 10–12

    cultural distinction of, 19–22

    descriptions of, 18–19

    geographical distribution of, *4*

    major entities in mythology of, *6*

    migrations of, 16–18

    origins of, 8–9, 13–14

    written caricatures of, 21

Center, Ronald, 91

Chadbourn, Mark, 88–89

Cilydd (Celtic king), 48, 65

The Coming of Cuchulain (Center), 91

Conall Cermach, 19, 28

Conchobhar (Celtic king), 53, 54

A Connecticut Yankee in King Arthur's Court (Twain), 94

Cruachan (band), 91

Cuchulain (warrior hero), 27, 28, 30, 53–56, *55, 90*

    in modern popular culture, 89–91

    supernatural ties of, 57–58

Culhwch (knight), 48, *49*

D

Danu (mother goddess), 33, 84

The Death of Cuchulain (Sheppard), 82

Deities, Celtic, human attributes of, 41

The Dream of Rhonabwy, 66–70, 93

Druids, 20–22, *22, 56*

Dun Aengus (hill fort), *23,* 23–24

Dwelling(s), of Celtic Iron Age, *25*

The Dying Gaul (sculpture), 81, *83*

E

Efnisien, 42, 44

Étaín (Irish princess), 38–40, *40*

F

Fairies, 34, *34*

The feast, 28

Fenian (Fionn) Cycle, 58–60

Fiana (Fenians), 58, 61–62

    initiation into, 60

Finegas (Druid), 59–60

Fingal's Cave (Mendelssohn), 58

Finn McCool, 59, *59,* 91

    See also Fionn mac Cumhaill

Fionn mac Cumhaill (Finn McCool), 58–60

Fomorians, 32–34, 88

Fuamnach (witch-goddess), 38–39

G

Galahad (Arthurian knight), 63, 83

Gaul, 10

ABOUT THE AUTHOR

Historian Don Nardo has written numerous acclaimed volumes about ancient and medieval civilizations and peoples. Among these are studies of the religious beliefs and myths of those peoples, including the Greeks, Romans, Egyptians, Sumerians, Celts, Germans, and others. Nardo also composes and arranges orchestral music. He resides with his wife, Christine, in Massachusetts.